Autumn on the Trail to Santiago

James Timberlake

authorHOUSE

AuthorHouse™
1663 Liberty Drive
Bloomington, IN 47403
www.authorhouse.com
Phone: 1-800-839-8640

© 2011 James Timberlake. All rights reserved.

No part of this book may be reproduced, stored in a retrieval system, or transmitted by any means without the written permission of the author.

First published by AuthorHouse 09/07/2011

ISBN: 978-1-4567-6690-0 (sc)
ISBN: 978-1-4567-6689-4 (hc)
ISBN: 978-1-4567-6691-7 (ebk)

Library of Congress Control Number: 2011907952

Printed in the United States of America

Any people depicted in stock imagery provided by Thinkstock are models, and such images are being used for illustrative purposes only.
Certain stock imagery © Thinkstock.

This book is printed on acid-free paper.

Because of the dynamic nature of the Internet, any web addresses or links contained in this book may have changed since publication and may no longer be valid. The views expressed in this work are solely those of the author and do not necessarily reflect the views of the publisher, and the publisher hereby disclaims any responsibility for them.

To my parents, Paul and Gertrude Roy Timberlake; to their parents, Wilbur and Casmire Jacmic Timberlake and Léo and Lucienne Poulin Roy; and to all my ancestors, in deep appreciation for this moment in tendriling time.

I would like to extend particular gratitude to my friend and landlady Maria Luísa Osorio. For the past ten years this bright little studio has been a refuge for me and for it I am profoundly grateful.

Additional Thanks and Acknowledgments to Jeff Timberlake; Melissa Oothout; Joe Torra; John Geannaris; Orlando Buzana; Deb Hickey; Ruth Scotch; Bob and Mary-Jo Sargent and the Staff at Flora Restaurant; Michael and Narayan Liebenson Grady and the Teachers at the Cambridge Insight Meditation Center; and for fueling my days - all the guys at Café Rustica in Somerville!

cover photograph of Église Saint Christaud by James Timberlake

author photograph by Deb Hickey

How easy it is to observe that a morning began with rain only to become sunny in the afternoon; that a pine tree stood at a particular place, or to note the name of a river bend. This is what people write in their journals. Nothing's worth noting that is not seen with fresh eyes. You will find in my notebook random observations from along the road, experiences and images that linger in heart and mind--a secluded house in the mountains, a lonely inn on a moor.

I write in my notebook with the intention of stimulating good conversation, hoping that it will also be of use to some fellow traveler. But perhaps my notes are mere drunken chatter, the incoherent babbling of a dreamer. If so, read them as such.

haiku master Matsuo Bashō, (1644-1694)

<u>The Knapsack Notebook</u>

All the stories I wrote were true... because I believed in what I saw. At the junction of the state line of Colorado, its arid western one, and the state line of poor Utah I saw in the clouds huge and massed above the fiery golden desert of eveningfall the great image of God with forefinger pointed straight at me through halos and rolls and gold folds that were like the existence of the gleaming spear in His right hand, and sayeth, Go thou across the ground; go moan for man; go moan, go groan, go groan alone go roll your bones, alone; go thou and be little beneath my sight; go thou, and be minute and as seed in the pod, but the pod the pit, world a Pod, universe a Pit; go thou, go though, die hence; and of this World report you well and truly.

Jack Kerouac

<u>On The Road</u>

Introduction

And so it goes... The journey once begun in <u>Sons of Thunder</u> continues on; same man, same spirit... blood, sweat and soul expressed out the same marrow but much has changed with the landscape, skyscape and timescape that inform the inscape of the Mind.

The eye-popping Whippit hit of June and July's Spain mellows now in the autumnal exhale reflected in cooling days, lengthening nights, and the repletion and harvest of agricultural labors along a string of trails spanning across southern France, over the Pyrénées, along the north of Spain and into Santiago for a second time this year.

While writing <u>Autumn on the Trail to Santiago</u> natural section breaks appeared in a way they did not in the flood-rush of <u>Sons of Thunder</u>. The initial 'On n'est pas riche mais on vie bien' segment is a toast to my family and to the love of food. 'Between the Rabbits' puts comestible brackets around le Chemin d'Arles, from Arles - through the lush landscapes of France - to the Pyrénées. 'Aragonia' describes el Camino Aragonés' descent out from the storm-ravaged Pyrénées into Spain, to reconnect with el Camino Francés in Puente la Reina. And 'Broken Water, Spanish Rain' is the long last leg of the journey; a dark wet trek down the metaphysical birth canal to Santiago, to the sea, and to the rest of life beyond this adventure.

on n'est pas riche mais on vie bien

journal - 8/3/06

yesterday's Spain feels like a dream-age ago away. that train from Hendaye stopped often... Bayonne, Biarritz - and the local summer fiestas are in full swing! people wearing white t-shirts and white pants with red bandanas wattle-knotted round their necks or pulled through belt-loops, all a-stroll and a-stand on the train station quays sliding by my tinted window. steep mountains and Easter green countrysides passing by, closeness blurry... slow precision far afield.

arriving in late-night Toulouse... stepped off the train and out of the station, got a cab to my hotel on Place Jeanne d'Arc - fat cabbie thought i was crazy for hiking 1100K. and despite my intention of going straight to bed... Dan at the bar - a 20 year old from Denver beginning his first couple-week tour of Europe. started talk of travel, the Camino, recovered from a slip into politics... 'one' turned to 'several' beers. we closed the hotel bar and went to an Irish pub for a whiskey and a Guinness i stopped him from slugging back before the black stout had finished settling beneath its creamy crown - i lived in Brighton for years and there are things one does not do. found an open kebab shop for a falafel gyro... famished from the fruit-snacked travel day. another European 4 a.m. pissing upside a sidewalk cement planter to the confoundation of tomorrow's dogs.

journal - 8/4/06

bought a French phone card and from a bustling carrousel-ed and café-ed plaza's 'France Télécom Bonjour' phonebooth i called my parents on their cell. they and my brother were actually en route to their flight out of Logan to Toulouse! so looking forward to our week together.

a mellow meditation in Cathédrale Saint Étienne... from a towering redwood-like center pillar radiates an odd, unsymmetrical combination of churchly buildings stitch-built together over a 600 year period of shifting architectural tastes and styles. the broadly embracing high-domed entry expanse masoned up against a more traditional three-naved temple... the walnut wood choir, dark with age and burnished-resin, where carved pagan and mythological figures dance Ad Majorem Gloriam Deum rondos and carolas... outer aisles alcoved with blue and red stained-glass chapels glowing Renaissance mind in the Roman umbra of thick stone walls. didn't care for the Basilica... couldn't get close to the altar where the most interesting painted ceilings were - gates and locks and chains. the Cathedral was open and more proudly outlandish!

with scent and sight enticements Toulouse invites exploration through its narrow pedestrian walkways lined with cafés, bars, boutiques, antiques, restaurants, pâtisseries, and kebab 'n fry shops. four-storied city canyon walls of copper, grey, and golden brick, or faced in soft stucco pastels. facades with wrought-iron twisted grille balconies... some brightly painted shutters latched against the sun... some casements merloned with stone balustrades brushed by lacy drapes... others open to an oriel-nooked breakfast table whose geranium, ivy or potted palm jitter in the breeze. pre-11H and post-18H... the familiar scene of double-fisted baguettes ambling by.

i decided to chow down tonight... a green salad with smoked duck breast, sliced sausage and the ubiquitous French mustard vinaigrette. if the French can't put mustard in their vinaigrette their pulses seize in mid-diastole. they're nice enough here to make me a half-portion of linguine carbonara, and the wood-oven roasted pizza is delicious with its sunny-side-up egg baked into the center! this place is hopping, and my 'understanding so much more than in Spain' francophone-tuned ear serpentines near tables' glassware, plates and bottles with the pleasure of comfortable recognition, and eaves-dropping.

journal - 8/5/06

woke early and brought my backpack to the hotel my parents had reserved. had a what the (!) $13 cup of coffee on Place de la Capitole. bought subs for the family and will soon head to the airport shuttle to pick them up!

……ten days later……
(silent movie piano playing pass-the-time melodies)

Thursday, August 15, 2006.

Subject: Sarlat-le-Canéda

Today being the 15th of August, and the Assumption, much of Arles is closed up tight. Remember from this country's perspective Jesus was a Frenchman. And Mary, in some foggy Arthurian past, was indeed the Queen of France. They just go along with that Bethlehem thing because it makes for a moving story.

Trained into Arles, a delightful 27°C after Grenoble's chill… What!? Grenoble!? I'll explain later. Opened to the 'Places to Stay' section in my Chemin d'Arles guide; first one's closed, second one's no answer, couldn't find the third so I barged, pissed-off-crumple-map-fisted, back to Place Voltaire to get my bearings - a room at Hôtel Voltaire! And it was Baby Bear juusst right. For 28 Euros I got a room and balcony kitty-cornered with two weathered wicker papasans overlooking a square whose sycamores shade the café table, chair, and umbrella clutter down below - a seine to the tanned strolling tourists. And with my smiling parents waving me off as the bus turned away from the Grenoble station in my heart and mind, I sat down to write about our week together in Sarlat…

La Vigne, the house we rented there, is tucked up above the medieval cité in an undriveably narrow rabbit warren of twisting cobbled streets; streets so narrow walking through them, arms extended, fingertips would soon turn red with geranium blooms, green with fern and potted hosta, and ochre from the soft golden stone of the buildings' outer walls. And polychrome hands down our favorite 'room' of the house was the small balcony giving onto a steeply pitched alpine range of clay-tiled and stone-chimnied roofs whose simple foreign beauty entranced us all... entranced us with the same fascination Monet had painting haystacks and Rouen Cathedral facades in the ever-shifting shadow/light play the different hours of the day played with our eyes and our contentment.

From the morning table piled with fruit, baguettes, croissants and chocolate almond pastry twists we scalloped with walnut cream bought from a local mill, or drizzled with dark amber chestnut-blossom honey wriggling from a wooden spoon...

From the afternoon table set out with olives, pickled onions, gherkins, local cheeses, charcuterie, and fried blood sausage... comparing duck and goose foie gras in states 'bloc pur,' 'terrine,' and 'paté' ...pork, rabbit, and fowl rillettes on crackers and croutons washed down with vins de Cahors, Bergerac, and Périgord...

From the evening table of marinated tomato and avocado salads, and grilled pink trout stuffed with sliced chorizo - so choice a bee converted from 'nectartarian' to mandible-saw a fat flake from the thin trout rib, six-leggedly grasp the morsel and churn hard working wings hive-ward away... over a clay-tiled alpine roof range.

...to a midnight table full of full white moonlight the crumbs of the day cast sated shadows upon.

As my grandfather used to say... as Pépère Léo Eugène Roy who worked long and arduous years in the Lewiston shoe mills used to say, "On n'est pas riche, mais on vie bien." 'We are not rich, but we live (eat) well...' reminding that real happiness comes from within only. How we celebrate what we have is the key. There was nothing more contented than that man's smile over a Father's Day picnic table's couple pecks of beer-steamed clams and his grandsons' buttery chins.

And I haven't mentioned restaurant food yet! Sarlat's stone streets are packed with cafés and restaurants whose kitchens must be pandemoniac Hells of duck and goose souls, so much 'product' passes through; restaurants glowing out mossy stone arches, clanking plates down narrow gaslit streets... tables budding to the eye and blooming on the tongue with salads arrayed with warm chèvre, walnuts, confit gizzards and smoked duck breast; scrambled eggs and omelets steeped in buttery cèpe jus; spicy tomato-mint soups garnished with twists of olive oil and cold cream; crisp confit de canard with duck fat and fines herbes roasted potatoes; Coquilles Saint Jacques - seared sea scallops bathed in herb cream and served in a crackling vol-au-vent well; foie gras stuffed quail; foie gras with onion jam; foie gras with truffles; seared duck breast with peach sauce; fruit and nut purée filled crêpes boozed with their corresponding fruit and nut liqueurs, then set ablaze... and back-of-the-spoon smacked crackling crust crème brulées.

My parents giggled like Christmas morning children while we savored some of these on a Rocamadour cliff-clung terrace facing sandy gold escarpments rising high above medieval church facades carved into the mountain stone. Facing these and looking up... a herd, (nothing of such size can be called a flock), a herd of fifteen-foot wingspan wide eagles riding the updrafts, circling above as if Delphically having found the exact center of the World.

Sarlat-le-Canéda expresses itself with Venetian carnival-mask changing faces. In summer fair fashion, street performers - jugglers, mimes, acrobats, clowns, the vibrantly sarapi-ed Peruvian flute band, and musicians busking through the south of France jamming bass, guitar, dulcimer and drum filled the night. Kaleidoscopic market day umbrellas flap and turn in the breeze bringing rotisserie chicken aromas... aromas of olive barrels and musk melons; plum, chestnut, walnut, paprika, garlic and herb flavored sausages of beef, boar, duck, and pork. The scents of ripe cow, goat, and sheep's milk cheeses aged in ash, oak leaf or fern; sweet sea-fresh crustaceans and fish on ice; the Irish ex-pat's brewer's malt, coffee roaster's grind, lavender sachets... inhaling past the belly to the toes and to the stone beneath them standing - so happy to be Earth's nose!

One night after a short hike by a massively walled-like-a-dam château and the walnut groves beyond; after a visit to Domme - a fortified bastide from the XIIth Century guarding the Dordogne River Valley below, a valley of sunflowers and deep green tobacco leaves undulant from the heights; after visiting La Roque Gageac - a shaving of a community whose homes' back walls are spackled against the mineral stained cliffs... whose terraced streets, for the sheltering river fog, are overgrown with tropical banana palms and all manner of frost-fearing blooms; after a winding country drive deep into vineyards for a winery tour and dégustation...

...After this and these - in the heart of Sarlat, in a small 800 year old lantern-lit courtyard where wrought-iron balconies and pastel shutters sculpt alate shadows upon these like golden canyon walls; into this courtyard the four of us made our way and sat among the many in attendance, rapt. Surrounded by upright bass, accordion, violin, and the goblet shaped darbuka drum whose various parts are whacked and rhythmed... Surrounded by these she stood so barefoot and beautiful, sable hair cascading, her Cleopatra black-lined eyes, Mediterranean dark olive skin - a Turkish diadem in memory's crown. If Edith Piaf's vocal horns could be multiplied, intensified, basso-ed and translated into Middle Eastern folk songs singing raw emotive rapture and melancholy, singing celebration, lamentation, and the mysteries the desert stars whisper to desert sands you'd hear this woman singing arms outstretched... fingers thrumming the air as if she played an ecstatic Cathedral organ deep within her core.

And through every image, phrase and gastronomic pleasure... through every thread and weave... family. Kitchen table family love and comfort in a foreign land. The needlessness to explain because we know; the uselessness of escape because we're here;

all we need to understand is present in flesh and bone. Be at home and so much idiocy falls away.

Didn't think I'd see Grenoble again, particularly not with my parents. But for the sake of taking advantage of the rapid French landscape change they decided, (after bringing my brother to the airport in Toulouse at the end of our week together), to head east and check out the Alps. And as my post-Sarlat destination is the historic Chemin trailhead in Arles, just south of Grenoble, I went with.

Grenoble, with its grey uniformity of building color, its ornate iron-work against carved stone dragons, lions, birds, and busts that garnish all buildings from banks to apartments, has the feel of a classic crumbled Vienna; of majesty, but a common majesty available to all citizens - and this with the JAGGED ALPS in the near offing.

Snow and glacier veined volcanic tors clung with mist, and clouds creeping across cliff sides with the slowness of something conscious of its own meditative pace. Thunder-high mountains, dramatically un-smoothed by erosion, whose molten youth can still be seen in the tree-ring-like stoney grain lines reaching across sheer rock faces. Following these grain lines with the eye the buckling of continental plates is clear... earthen birth throes' visible echoes. Having trekked up into the Mercantour National Park on the French / Italian border about four years ago, I encouraged my parents to head down to explore those jaw dropping heights... and I, I headed south into Provence.

The last night in Sarlat I dreamt of Mickey. Pépère's cousin and his wife, Uncle Lucien and Aunt Jeanne, lived next door to me growing up and their dog Mickey was a friend in my childhood. In my dream he was old, crooked of spine, and fatter than memory recalls but it was him. Rumbling on the bus to Arles, dwelling on the dream - he was the first pilgrim I knew in my 'don't cross the street' bound youth. In those pre-leash-law days Mickey could roam far and free, all the way to the Mecca of Dairy Joy where he'd waggingly wait for someone to drop an ice cream cone. It was an amazement to me then how he could find his way home... the quiet backyard ways he knew. He's long dead now. Uncle Lucien and Aunt Jeanne have died and their house next door has been sold twice. My parents are reaching the ranks of the older people on the street... and I'm off waiting for ice creams to fall from a summer sky before finding my way home.

    Jim

> may we have ease of mind;
>   may we have comfort of heart;
>   may our lives be peaceful lives.
>   ~the buddha

journal - 8/15/06

i'd love an ape-clan grooming... a haircut and close beard trim.

yeah, the Assumption. the Holy Hoovering of Mary up to celestial heights that the body who bore the Christ would not know the defilements of death... like there is anything unholy in mud, muck, dung and flesh-rot. as most everything downtown and historic is closed for this holiday i headed well out to city outskirt cloverleaf exchanges and to the Géant Shopping Center whose roadside billboards bark in DayGlo phrases that it will be open on the 15th. this one's getting full and i'm in search of a new journal. on the way back i bypassed the Alyscamps but could not go in. too weird to walk away from a modern shopping plaza then tour an ancient necropolis.

got a guide-map at the tourist office. sat at Van Gogh's actual Café la Nuit... an incensed Frenchman yelling at waiter and boss! sent his food back three times because he got pasta instead of potato or potato instead of pasta with his plat du jour. he's probably still tormented by the starch. a crowd of Japanese tourists sat down. waiters expressing to the universe and all there-in how hard they're trying to be patient - thinking that masks their masks of indignation.

went to a Picasso / Goya / Doré exhibit themed 'Bulls and Minotaurs.' Picasso's eleven stage deconstruction of the Bull was incredible... from rough hewn sketches, to precise representation, to geometrically cracked fantasia - with a pivoting twirl or two in the center of the room it becomes phantasmagoric. and through some acid-wash process he created seemingly ink-blotted, but meticulously precise, haiku-like bullring scenes... bulls, picadors, toreadors, spectators. i'm fascinated by the fullness of expression within the simplest of lines. never been inspired to draw before but i bought two waxy pencils and drew my balcony overlooking Place Voltaire... not bad. and as happens in zennist attention - i lost track of time entirely and found myself calmed and soothed.

a lot of downtime - Santiago, Pamplona, Sarlat-le-Canéda, Arles... sadly, my calluses have softened and my feet are ripe to blister and bleed all over again. but so it goes. i'm excited to drift through cicada-ratcheting orchestrations again, to feel the earth treadmill turn again beneath my feet but i seem to be having a hard time getting started on my way. i've come so far... now another 1600K yawns before me. no wonder i feel like sitting... eating aioli, tapenade, and gnawing lavender stalks... getting fat and listening to cicada songs in Provence.

journal - 8/16/06

had fun drawing the mirrored, piped and windowed sink-corner of the room last night. so many textures.

went to the post office. as it was closed yesterday the morning line was long, but the teller was friendly. mailed my Spanish journals home with a prayer of arrival.

short-cropped haircut. will see how it grows out. Euro hair isn't like mine. i sensed she was uncertain with what to do with my blond straw but faked it well enough. noticed beneath the shears how poor my French has become. comprehension is there but speaking is fragmented staccato... not flowing at all. since Pamplona i've mainly been in English mode... not cerebrally or conversationally challenging the foreign language muscle in the brain.

an eccentrically dressed woman plopped down next to me at my afternoon café, café crème and International Herald Tribune. her dog twisted its leash asphyxiatingly around the table legs and she, from a Mary Poppins bottomless carpet bag, lifted out what looked like a bovine thigh bone and thud it down at her feet for him to gnaw...

...which reminds me... i haven't been recording food in Arles! and the night before last was a delight! a Provençal vegetable terrine... oily, herbed, and well-packed. spicy Provençal fish soup... i'm digging the accompanying crouton plate with dense rouille and grated cheese - each in their own miniature crock. duck confit is meltingly tender... herbs and seasonings reaching deeply into the meat, a caramelized onion and anchovy filled choux and a roasted stuffed tomato garnish the plate. a selection of chèvres and a Calvados finish out the meal... echoes of orchard and field.

last night - a salade Périgourdine... lettuce and tomatoes dressed with the usual mustard vinaigrette and topped with lardons, smoked duck breast slices, walnuts and confit gizzards. an assiette Camargue... bull sausage and bull crétons with olives and gherkins. an assiette Aïoli with sharply garlick-ed mayonnaise, court bouillon poached escargot and calamar rings, hard-boiled eggs and tender salt cod. what a dish! and a crème caramel to close.

grinning anticipation for tonight's meal... tucking in and tucking to. couldn't get in this restaurant a few nights ago and the receptionist seemed to appreciate my second attempt to dine here when i made my reservation this morning. how can there be but one waitress for all this! and she's the receptionist too! and i'm betting the chef's wife.

what a feast is unfolding on the tongue... Noix de Saint Jean - a fortified red wine apéritif steeped with green walnut fruit, vanilla, cinnamon and clove. white truffle raviolis with mushroom cream and grated cheese. i had better eat slowly. i haven't seen that family of four across the way get a scrap of food since before my apéritif and wine débouchement. a 2000 Domaine de Pourra Gigondas was débouched. the wine's a full Rhône... tobacco, tannins, pepper and spice - brief burn. how can there be just one server?! this woman is sweet but she's giving the worst service i've ever seen... ever. and not for me, i don't care. but a 20 minute wait for the beer at the table to my left... the four-top is done with apps and still have no wine... the family of five still hasn't had a thing cleared - it must be 40 minutes now. the patience is astounding. scallops wrapped in bacon - skewered, grilled and balsamic washed - would have been better as a reduction but my palate isn't weeping. cassoulet looks crispy - let's try. Hosanna and Huzzah! a salty fatty sausagey breadcrumb-crusty ducky beany wonder! ripe room-warm cheeses... a tarte tatin with crème anglaise on the way. dying tonight i'll die smiling.

loudly liquidly sucking bouillabaisse liquor out a spiny pink shrimp carapace... my table neighbor relishes a tomato-saffron broth spattered white tableclothed meal.

silky wind-billowed clouds waving inland from storming southern seas exhale humid breezes well into the night, dewing beads on leaf and carved lintel scrolls. a full belly and a balcony and i am crowned king.

journal - 8/17/06

drew the sink-corner again. variations and improvements on a theme... slept late - i'm sluggish with the humidity. no rain, but high winds are snapping sere sycamore leaves from stem nodes and blowing them down the streets like loudly tumbling packie brown paper bags.

Alyscamps was impressive. the long tomb-lined road to the repository of Saint Genesius - martyr. an iconic raggedy-feathered old mourning dove paces a crackt stone sarcophagus, purring shallow coos with each panted breath. she marks the start of tomorrow's peripatetic ways, not the empty temple. scent and sound of wind whipped cedars, silence of ancient stone tombs...

called the gîte privée. calling ahead to reserve a bed is the way here in France... just showing up at the albergue door is the way in Spain. nervous about phone comprehension. not being able to see the others' lips move worries me, but the woman spoke clearly and kindly.

there's an amphitheater in the center of Arles. after the fall of Rome, the locals ripped out the seating and within the arcaded walls, now an instant stronghold, they built rings of homes and businesses. i saw a postcard of an XVIIIth Century woodcut depicting Arles like this.

Place Forum. restaurant beside this café with the sidewalk-blocking burner and trough-pan bubbling a paella an occasional white aproned cook or casual passer-by stirs with a wooden peel... kitchen up on the second floor has a window-hung cowbell the chef hammers hard with an aluminum ladle when a table's plates are ready... sometimes he just yells. having a beer here watching odd, loin-clothed and face-painted 'Native Americans' noodling zamphir chant music against their boom-box's thumping techno sounds. a few days ago i saw the same flautist who performed on the plaza before the Palais des Papes in Avignon! what - seven years ago?! he was here with the same pre-recorded background accompaniment... the same Ave Maria repertoire. i recognized the sound of him from around a corner but didn't trust ear until the eye confirmed.

forgot about considering this place tucked off Place Forum on my earlier restaurant searches. La Grignotte. another place with husband / chef and one wife / waitress. a little polygamy would smoothen things out. fortified peach wine in a chiseled glass to start. a tin of fleur de sel on the table. crisp-fried eggplant slices petaled out with a coarse ratatouille in the center arrives first. same Gigondas as last night. i'm getting fat! fish soup comes again in a tureen piled round with croutons and mini-crocks of rouille and grated cheese. this is the best fish soup of my life. the fleur de sel is up front on the tongue and as it glides down the throat all the flavors of fish, shellfish, fennel and saffron follow reined in dog-team style, racing palate and tongue - the best! i may have one for dessert. now a plate of creamy sliced potatoes and lapin à la lavande et romarin... tobacco-y Gigondas going so well with the lavender stuck in my roasted rabbit crammed teeth. someone's cell phone just went off with the 20th Century Fox fanfare...

between the rabbits

Thursday, August 17, 2006.

Subject: Arles

On the shelves of our rented home-away-from-home in Sarlat-le-Canéda I found a fated book called <u>The Art of Pilgrimage</u>, by Philip Cousineau. Within, it offered the following definition... "Pilgrim: an early derivation from the Latin 'per agrum' - through the field... a curious soul who travels beyond known boundaries, crosses fields, touches the earth with a destination in mind, with a purpose in heart... who longs to endure a difficult journey to reach a sacred center of his or her world - a place made sacred by saint, hero, or god." Nothing to add to that, is there? And after a Zen quote, "Don't get even, get odd," he elaborates on many pilgrim destinations from Graceland, City Lights Books, Allen Ginsberg's Howling New York City room, to the warehouse with the biggest ball of rubber bands in the world... all bearing the same mark of folly for baby it ain't the destination, it's the ride. And my ride's churning like a 1880's Mississippi River steamboat, furnace-belly full of red hot coal.

Unbeknownst to me, Arles, like Rome, is one of those places I've always avoided. Just too much jam-packed history! It overwhelms and aches me brain. Days can be spent exploring the five historic and cultural paths that wind through Old Arles... paths highlighting Roman antiquity monuments (1), Medieval carved archways and facades (2), Renaissance (3) and Classical architecture (4), and an exploration of Van Gogh's presence here (5). I actually had coffee and a Ricard at his 'Café la Nuit.' They were fresh out of absinthe. During the last few years of his life Van Gogh painted over 300! canvases here. The Dutch were invading the south of France even then. And just to slap the tourists silly and squish their art appreciating acumen through a sieve, there's currently an exhibition of 50 photographers in 50 different sites strewn about municipal, historic, and private homes. Too much... just too much.

As I don't have a proper tourist guide with thorough information I'm gleaning what I can from placards, postcards, and stolen moments reading a paragraph or two from bookstore histories. So...

...Once upon a really wicked long time ago, there were hunter-fisher communities on these Rhône River delta islets. As the islets grew through sedimentation, so grew the outposts into important trade points for Lebanese fishermen, Phoenician sailors and the Greeks since this location facilitated intercourse between Italy and Spain. The Celts were here by 6 B.C. and their nomenclature Ar-Laith, 'the land of marshes,' was romanized into Arelate. When Marseilles, (ancient Marsilia), sided with Pompeii against Julius Caesar, the aid Arelate gave Caesar's soldiers was rewarded with admission into the Empire as a Roman City and, as a Roman City, Roman tradition seeped in.

Roman tradition forbade the burial of corpses within city limits. This observation of sanitary ways led to a solemn form of ancestral awareness and respect as axis roads radiating out from the city were lined with tombs. One progressed from the wilderness, through a cemetery, into the living heart of a city; the metropolis surrounded by the necropolis.

At some point Arles' necropolis, the Alyscamps, became the most prominent in the Mediterranean world, and being an honored place of burial certain Paleo-Christian martyred saints' bones were reposited here; the bones of Saint Genesius, a Roman civil servant beheaded for refusing to persecute the Christians; the bones of Saint Trophimus, the first Bishop of Arles whose funeral, according to lore, was attended by the Christ whose kneeling knee imprinted the episcopal sarcophagus' lid. As the popularity of devotional cults within Christianity grew in the first millennium, (the cult of Mary, of Saint James the Thaumaturge, of Saints Peter and Paul), Arles became an important stop on the road to Santiago de Compostela... between Rome and Galicia... a stomping ground and point of holy departure for those hat, cloak, staff, and shell bearing wanderers on their way to the Finisterre sea.

It is from here I take Lao Tze's single step that starts the journey of a thousand miles; in the scent and sound of wind-churned cedars and the silence of cracked stone sarcophagi, like Orpheus down a Dantean chanted road of the dead I start another old road... traveling beyond known boundaries and crossing fields on the way to the sea - and I am very excited.

>Jim

> may we have ease of mind;
> may we have comfort of heart;
> may our lives be peaceful lives.
> ~the buddha

journal - 8/18/06

drew the sink-corner again last night to the disintegrate sounds of hard rain shredding against papery sycamore leaves. woke to resplendent blue skies and headed over to the corner grocer for fruit and a... the 'Dan-up' yogurt drink in Spain has shifted mark to 'Yop,' here in France. went to my morning café, ordered a café crème and pain au chocolat but was served an espresso and a croissant, (hmmm). wound down to the Alyscamps... caisse closed - ha!

the attendant woman, 'la responsable,' was there in the ticket kiosk when i left. asked for an initiatory 'tampon,' (the 'sello' in Spain - the pilgrim's passport stamp that marks the étapes), and gave her a few Euros for a coffee or a glass of wine. confusion rippled across her face. said i wanted to start the Chemin with a symbol and confusion shifted to smile.

the trail zigzagged uselessly through streets i knew well enough to bee-line straight through. crossed the bridge over the Rhône to the other side's neighborhoods and commercial centers, to a rotary's offshoot that shot a narrow lane out into the Camargue... out into sprawling marshlands dried to plains by a tight network of channels irrigating rice and cereal grains... the famed bone-grey stallions grazing... fifteen-foot high roadside reeds walling me in. so invigorating to be hiking again. fresh! a man fueled by sun and the far horizon. passed by a manse or two but through no village all day.

vicious mosquitoes on the road for the marshland's incubation and plump horse-flesh blood reserves.

after the freshly painted truss bridge... an open café-bar-traffic-round-a-bout area full of tanned, sandaled, and wind flappingly loose clothed vacationers. a colorful canopied campground nearby - a coconut aloe skin scent on the warm wind... a simple summer hangout feel in the air.

headed up into Saint-Gilles-du-Gard and as the tomb-lined day began it ended with a well-dressed funeral processing into the transfigurant church... a human life morphing in the human minds who, for now, remain. the golden church facade seems tremblingly alive between her three archivolted blood-red doors and the blue Provence sky.

sat down at a café that ended up being the key-keeper to the place i had reserved... Gîte la Maison Camarguaise. this older couple owns the café / bar / restaurant. the rundown house next to is what they rent out... oddly, like an elderly grandmother's abode. fusty and quaint and lace arm-rested with faded chrysanthemum-and-rose wallpapered walls, cupboard shelves sagging with the weight of piled plates long-gone company used to use, mullioned casement windows, linoleum kitchen tile corners lifting up as if allergic to the floor, a sink pipe bent phallic out a crumbling stone wall... the dusty sweet scent another century's dry furniture respires. upstairs, a claw-foot tub with a spattering shower and no curtain. i'll have to root around to find a mop to swab the floor.

a meander through concentric streets... light stucco and crossbeam constructed buildings, residential and not much aside from the church to shoot, draw, or dwell upon. main-drag tabac-presse shops and bars. somewhat run-down. this is the bohemian summer south and that French 'pride in appearances' sensibility is also on vacation.

municipalities like these commonly offer a 'base de loisirs' ...a 'leisure base,' an inexpensive place to camp or rent a caravan for the week and use as a hub for day excursions, alternating history and art exposure in Arles, Avignon or Aix-en-Provence with horseback riding, canoeing, ocean, sport and sun... for nights of card games and carousing, a sandy floored wall-less disco for the kids to get sexed up and ensure the future its taxes. what an opportunity... this ability to vacation so cheaply in such beauty, eat such food and absorb such depth of art and history simply because Art and History are there, present and alive.

in the tobacco shop, a woman in front of me... her shaggy dog loved my feet and was lapping, rubbing pink jowls and rolling his back on my ticklish toes and arches... cracking me up.

a warm reception in the Saint Gilles church. 'You're a pilgrim? No charge to visit the crypt.' she stamped my credencial and directed me towards the gate. the dim crypt was incredibly spacious for the weight of the church above and descending i felt like Bela Lugosi on the stairs. apparently, Gilles was a Greek Christian hermit who withdrew deep into the forest and spent years in ultimate solitude... his only companion, a doe, who sustained him on her milk. in the same way the children left Narnia chasing a stag, Gilles' retreat was discovered by the king's hunters while they were in pursuit of the wet-nursing doe. they shot, but wounded the hermit with their arrows instead. impressed by his humility, King Wamba, in apologia, bestowed on Gilles a tract of land where he built for him a monastery... and for his wounds he became the Patron Saint of cripples. his shadowy recessed tomb is tossed with dusty flowers, dusty photos, dusty canes and crutches, dusty shells and walking staffs.

came back to the café to eat. she made me a salad, a tuna filled red pepper, and a filet of whitefish wrapped with smoked salmon slices over pasta in a béchamel... a carafe-let of wine... sweet gaufrettes with pistachio ice cream. chatting, she mentions the Camargue is over with the crossing of the Petit Rhône and tomorrow should be through hills and vines. 7 Place République - she's retiring at the end of the year.

two Germans staying at the gîte i must have overlooked came by looking for food. she wasn't serving. closing up after i finished. they want to make it to Santiago in six weeks! no way in hell is that gonna happen marquees behind my eyes. "O good luck with that!" on my lips. Wolfgang with the Dostoyevskian beard... the other has been to Boston.

the café couple asked me to double lock the door when i bedded down for the night - "Faut pas tenter le Diable!" 'No need to tempt the Devil.' and from my bedroom window i sketched the church in the dark.

8/18/2006
Alyscamps' Roman sarcophagi moored
    to the dark domed Saint Honorat nave ~
wind churned cedar scent
    and carved stone silence hold,
        as crystal pool water palm-bowled to the lips,
            one tatter-rag feathered mourning dove who
raspily purr-coos each agèd bird breath shifting
    prehistoric feet upon a time-pocked and
        time-smoothed crackt crypt ~
who tilts one bead-bright eye to the shimmering blue sky,
    who hears my footsteps grind gravel away...
        nunc dimittis servum tuum.

8/18/2006

plumed pampas reeds whisper,
   white egret wings ~
      the deep blue cobalt sky.

      *

a simple road winds
   the Camargue marsh plains ~
jewel lustrous dragonflies
   break wishbone copulation
      to hover wonder at me walking here
   and i agree...
listening to sole pads once again swell hot blisters ~
   the same lime-gold lichens
      streaming down Santiago Cathedral spires gild
         stone farm chimneys, their clay-tile roofs,
            and dead garrigue shrub-wood walking here.

      *

commanding 'get thee the hell
   outta my ear, mosquito-demon...'
      from the thick reeds, one sapphire
      dragonfly drops a venom-stunned grasshopper
         offering at my feet.

      *

   glass marble clacking
      cricket song
   fills the overturned blue bowl sky.

journal - 8/19/06

my sweet, kind, slowly speaking lady - sometimes i just don't get around to getting names - she left me a petit déjeuner on the table: tea packets, fruit juice, crackers, croissants, butter and jams. learned it got light earlier than i thought under my dark Place Voltaire sycamore arbors. and i was right about the house. it belonged to a deceased mother. the daughter lives in Marseilles and 'Sweet-Kind-Slow' manages it.

padded soft steps out of the quiet stone town and soon into vineyards upon gravel roads... upon gravel roads threading through orchards of nectarine and peach with high reeds rattle-lining irrigation waterways. the nectarine trees have a buzz-cut look to them. wonder if that pruning technique better lets the sunlight in or emancipates the fruit more freely to the harvest?

like the hesitant pattering of cloud-front scattered rain drops come the infrequent cicadas, soon thickly filling the air. i love their ratcheting song... fell long in love with it in the sage-and-thyme scented olive groves of the Peloponnesus.

followed a line of light green pinion pines down into Vauvert. the couple who helped me with directions said the center was in fiesta-mode and bulls were coming running through... buzzing loudspeakers blare classical bull music marches and a few blank fireworks boom. sewer grates were covered with plastic tarp and sand to prevent taurine shins from snapping... but i didn't see any, neither hoof nor horn.

Vauvert was the highlight of the day. stopped at a shaded café for a coffee and Pernod, rummaged for my pencils and began to draw the fountain. a kid came by... called his two friends over... 'Wow! You did that! You have more?' absolutely nothing in the world like a child's praise... even if the thing itself is crap. birds sculpted on the fountain edge came out surprisingly well. hardest part is the geometry, math, and setting up the sizes - the rest is shading. a pleasant difficulty. a relaxed mood leaving Vauvert... the mellow zen rest of the fountain.

to Gallargues-le-Montueux the trail was about 80% on the road... blisters beginning.

had difficulty finding the gîte in this steep town. Saturday afternoon, all is closed down, streets vacant. no one to ask. eventually called Irène, the woman posted on the Mairie, (Town Hall), door as the off-hours 'responsable' for the gîte, and she met me on the square. so friendly and so helpful and so informative - but so unaware. i sat there in my sweat and stink as she talked about all the places to stay from here, across France, to Somport! by 17:30H i hadn't showered, laundered, or written a line. two other pèlerins here as well... long grey-blond haired Natalie and the 72-year-old guy.

after ablutions, at last! wanted to write and draw... nope. should have read the signs upon arrival. should have known when i finally sat down at the bar overlooking once dazzling rooftops around the square, and the light had gone grey and undefined, that it was not going to be about my will tonight. the Germans, Wolfgang and Tussen, came by craving beers and we talked long. Tussen has the same inner thigh problem i have and i learned the German slang for 'crotch rash' is kleine wulfje - 'a little wolf' - love that. they sang in the Église Saint Gilles crypt this morning before leaving. a sonorous start to the day.

stomach grumbling around 21H. went back to the multi-purpose gîte / music school / gymnastics center. Natalie and Old Guy were already bedded down. the Germans took their sleeping bags and spent the night out on the indoor / outdoor plastic-grass-carpeted patio. as quietly as possible i made beans with tomato and onion, and helped myself to the olive oil there. for the sake of quietude i put the pot and dishes in the oven to be washed in the morning.

8/19/2006

a stop to piss in cornstalk leaves ~
   left look look right looking
      for the bug-beast making that bzzzzzzzzzzz
         with flesh so tender a-dangle and bait-jigged
           in the breeze.

    *

Black High-Tension Power Lines slung hot summer low
   crackle nape hair,
      wrist down and pubes ~
  wondering on urinic conduction
     and the Weekly World News...
        walking energetically away.

8/19/2006

Camargue irrigate rice plains,
   towering reed beds, white egret flares,
      dust bathing bone-grey horses scratching spines, roll bold
         bellies
   and swipe skull-crush hooves high,
      raising billow incense dust clouds
         to the divine blue Midi sky...
   all left behind as bridge stones
      into new minded lands ~

    *

swole-red-mosquito smacked wrist...
   bloodstain bathed away but
      i bear the enduring mark of Cain ~

    *

    far field cypress lines pulse
        black to lime
            black to lime
                black to lime
    and back to deep green again under
        the sunbeam juggling clouds ~

        *

smooth almond fruit crackt carapace casings...
    a summer-baked nut within.
        wild olives shimmer.
    donkey brays rattle silvery-green broom twigs
        and brown seedpods.
hillside orchard's black opal nectarines shine over
        gnarly grapevine trunks
    swelling powder-blue fruit clusters...
        some grape beads burnished window-to-the-soul bright
            by breeze nodding leaves.

        *

    this... and that much more.
one full breath in the sudden silence
    one cicada makes at my footstep's pause beneath
        her pinion pine
            reverses the stain
        back to Eden again.

journal - 8/20/06

part of Irène's diatribe yesterday was warnings regarding the entry to and the exit from Montpelier. 'The Chemin is poorly marked in the garrigue, (the dense sea-coastal scrubland), and the Nationale is completely excavated with new road construction, so walk most of the way then take the bus.' it felt a bit fraudulent to take the bus, but a couple K out of 1600 isn't bad. i imagine medieval pilgrims hopped a mule cart or two.

following the signs through Lunel to Lunel Viel... all throughway walking walking by cement strip-mall stores, garden centers, swimming pool installations, stacked patio bricks and paving-stone canyons... until the road to Saint-Geniès where i picked up the Chemin again - a soft, pine and oak scented trail with the Nationale not far off rumbling. hating it practices hate, object of meditation practices meditation.

passed several creepy 'Texas Chainsaw' caravan areas with rusted out half-barrel grills, and i don't see the pots for pissing in. i think they're tapping electricity directly from the cables overhead. no one around. i almost expect to hear strings of metatarsal wind chimes clattering.

dry heat kicking up but i felt strong beneath the pack. mistook Baillargues for Vendargues and am annoyed with myself. i've done this before. regardless of the mirages anticipation brings, you are never hiking ahead of the game! no kiddo, you were not magically transported an hour ahead while you rested five minutes in the shade.

at last in Vendargues... modern, planned-out characterless suburbs - a Montpelier bedroom community. many families in shaded backyards enjoying Sunday afternoon grilled food, milky tumblers of pastis in their non-cigaret holding hands. the bus to Montpelier passes at 14:30H and i arrived just after 13H.

sat and had a coffee and pastis myself. hardly finished half of each before the boss started piling up chairs and tables... closing up for the August break. the plaza's dry fountain gathering leaves... bar now closed, too... a corner grocery closes... discarded fish-scaley ice clinks meltingly against hot curbstones. the wind pushing dry leaves and the meat shop's ex-utero cooler compressor are the only other sounds - no voices, no traffic, no window music or clanking plates... eerie. napped on a shaded bench. paranoia tangles my leg around a backpack shoulder strap.

big toe is caterwauling... sharp penetrating pain every step, every time the inner boot bears down on the nail. i think there's a sub-nail cyst swelling.

Montpelier. hard to get an immediate feel for the city on a Sunday afternoon... spacious pedestrian streets, some expansive polished stone squares like Place de la Comédie surrounded by ornately sculpted XVIIIth Century classical architecture, cafés, the bedazzling-danceball of a Carrousel, and the Fountain of the Muses - green ferned and mossy among all this stone... the steel wheel-to-rail city trams squeal-rumbling through it all. Comédie ends in a tree-shaded bluff overlooking the modern city below - opposite to where Église Sainte Anne's white stone steeple strikes against blue arched skies. radiating out from Comédie the pedestrian boulevard edges are blanketed in bazaar fashion with southern boheems weaving bracelets and paste-jeweled trinkets... coal black Africans with their leather-ware and whittled wooden dolls' dangling penises bobbing on bouncy springs.

filthy cheap hotel... crusty black panties and cigaret butts litter a closet shelf above the hangars.

this is going to be a hard journey. so far - a lot of asphalt. and all Irène's talk about gîtes and places to stay... do i take that to mean lodging will be sparse? Montpelier is another city i want to enjoy but doing so will interrupt the flow of the Chemin before it even starts to flow... fingernails on chalkboards, the teacher's topic moot.

got some spectral night shots of Place de la Comédie's dramatically lit stone facades and their reflections upon the polished plaza. hit the Irish bar and the Jameson's hit me back. Irish ex-pats here teaching English were typically story-tellingly hysterical - holy NASCAR! they talk fast. back in the room i drew the open window shutter-wings as the sky went lighter blue with early dawn.

journal - 8/21/06

strolled into amazement approaching the Cathédrale Saint Pierre! gargantuan pillars holding up an incredibly high stone-canopied archway... all that mammoth stone up in the air! so hulking and elevated it evokes the discombobulation of a whale pirouetting on one fluke tip. standing beside the pillars i looked and felt like a wee wee pigeon, oui, oui. steady mellow meditation inside those solid Cathedral walls... outside, drew the facade... learned a few things. went uptown and drew Église Saint Roch... learned a few things. the Vauvert fountain came out nicely because i did the pencil-tip perspective measuring. here, i'm self-conscious about being a caricature with his thumb out so the result is skewed... days are days and nights are nights.

while drawing, drunk Abdul came over and wanted me to imbibe. he kept praising the wine. i kept wondering how many times that battered plastic wine bottle's been refilled, and with what. 'Life is hard when you don't work,' he repeats. 'so work!' i think. probably not so simple. he asked. i gave. he said, 'God bless.' in the as yet unwritten <u>Poor Jimmy's Almanack</u> read, " 'Tis better to pay for a pauper's blessing than to get a fat priest's benediction for free."

i wonder if i'm fighting the Chemin? wonder why i feel like my wagon is thumping along on square wheels? France is not Spain - now is not the same, or even a similar, trail experience and i find myself imposing intentions on a trail that scoffs at these.

unanchored... ungrounded... rootless... rankled by Christians' condescending 'Members Only' smiles... their frenetic pack rat stock-piling of 'looked at' or 'touched upon' relical flotsam. "Êtes-vous croyant?" comes the question. meaning, are you a believer? and my response is, sure. i believe that with practice, meditation liberates the heart and mind from hatred, fear, greed, and anger. 'O that's just philosophy not religion.' what? and the sky is blue. rancor is nothing but hot salt on an open wound. a wound the i-me-my mind myself probably opened. salt falling upon Integrity would not even be noticed. i think i'd like to spend another day here. maybe metaphysically restart the Chemin.

journal - 8/22/06

late stay in bed. dreamt Mt. Washington erupted.

i think it was a fitting idea, this one more day... if for nothing else than realizing, remembering and dwelling upon how quickly what i've learned dissipates and that the 'work' continues to be returning the mind to Now.

wanted to start the day with a meditation at Église Saint Roch but didn't care for the feel there. instead i drew for a few butt-numbing hours at the château d'eau where the bygone aqueduct used to conduit into the city. also played with perspective while drawing the plane trees and the curving park's balustrade leading away to the Église Sainte Anne steeple in the distance. seeing things in disappearing focal lines with shaded shapes within is weird. finished up by doing a free-form château d'eau which was 'détente' for mind and hand... just scratch it out without worry. we used to practice this in tai chi class. doing a loose and carefree form after a class of precise attention to detail is mentally unbinding before going on with the day. went back to the Cathedral plaza for a coffee and another sketch of the j-awe dropping portico. not working out so well. since the notebook paper is small maybe i should be working on a smaller angle or aspect... take a part for the whole. perhaps that's why the fountain came out. it wasn't a monumental facade. wish i had taken that sumi-e class and knew which lines to choose.

the tales of Saint Roch reveal him to be a medieval physician.

healing so many plague victims while making a pilgrimage to Rome, it was said the pestilence fled upon his mere approach. when he contracted the disease himself he retreated into the forest and built a hut of branches. God bubbled up a spring for him to drink from but it was the anadrome that saved his life... a dog found him, brought bread to his lean-to and licked his wounds until they healed. this image is his ecclesiastic iconography - a man opening his robe to expose a raw leg lesion, beside him a dog holds out a small brown loaf in its mouth. in childhood's 'genius' my Mom stuck a knife in an electric outlet and scorched the palms of her curious hands. the family dog became obsessed with her burns and licked them into prompt and scarless healing. dust motes in pellucid time dancing. i'm finding an affinity is opening up to these saints with animal familiars. wondering if the early tale-shapers were schooled in Greek myth or if it was simply the pastoral nature of the age?

stopped in at the Cangeceiros Exhibition in the gallery on Place de la Comédie. from the Sertão in northeastern Brazil... bloodthirsty wasteland bandits and die-hard blood brothers, they reigned the plains from 1926 to 1938 when their leader was killed with many of his band. they were beheaded - their heads, hats, clothes, weaponry, cartridge belts... their whole kit was put on tour from estate to estate and from city to city. heads touring with toothpick-propped-open eyes for the grotesque swelling. photographed with the locals... tied to prison bars and corral boards... sometimes even on church steps they were displayed with pomp and pride.

journal - 8/23/06

so i awoke and had at it. following Irène's advice to not walk out of Montpelier i took the tram to the sprawling-lawned suburban bus station for a connection to Grabels. man waiting for the bus... older, greyish, southern French healthy ease... has a son in Thailand, travel repartée. an amiable start. a fresh restarting.

asked the bus driver if Grabels was the last stop. again - so friendly and helpful. he drove off-route to show me where the church was, knowing the bridge i needed crossed the river down below it. ate a palmier... not quite on par with the one from Saint-Gilles - good god of my belly! i don't think i mentioned that oven-warm pâtisserie glowing soul of the quiet morning town. the pastry wedges splayed out like a star... sooo caramelly crispy - each bite a yin / yang, feathery / crackling rapture.

picturesque church-sycamore-plaza-blue-sky composition i crisscrossed several times looking for that elusive bridge. a steep start to a high plain. abnormally vocal horses at a sprawling hillside stable estate. blue-white streaked mountains beyond for the limestone cliffs and ozone-y distance. this crumbly limestone doesn't hold much soil or produce lush forests, but rather sparse and spackled tree growth letting the sun-bleached white schist shine through.

disconcerting feelings early on. i kept wondering if i had died? the tram and bus rides to unknown places, the two helpful guides - Jim Jarmusch 'Dead Man'-like. and a deep, dizzyingly inner ear silence... except for a few flies buzzing, which only enhanced the sensation. it felt trans-dimensional. and i don't know why Irène thought Grabels was a dangerous place. she warned us to watch out and watch our wallets, etc... but that again made me feel like i was on a plane somewhere different than expected.

Montarnaud is another modern sprawl plotted out with pre-planned neighborhoods... 'lotissements,' they're called. Public Works workers at the hedges with shears - 'Compostelle? That way!' smiling like the Cathedral is just over the hill.

didn't stop until the café in Aniane where i filled my bottle with tap-water so cold the plastic opaqued and sweat. had a brie sandwich and a tea. chewing on interconnection, reciprocity, symbiosis...

a desire to introspect and soothe and balance often needs to be invited to arise.

a spectacular mountain trail! never seen earth that deep coppery red before. never! the maroon trail ribboning through green trees, under blue sky, the pine-plumed white schist mountains behind... passed a pèlerin sleeping in the shade. he never stirred. thought i might see him pass by later, but no. never saw him again. should have looked for an axial ankle pulse throbbing.

starting at my rest in and well-after Aniane... the steady wail of emergency vehicles racing somewhere away. as i trudged the gorge rim the road follows, Pont du Diable ahead (from the XIth Century!) ...the clustered cars there, the people, the name - thought for certain someone had gone off a cliff but it was just Sunday crowds swimming and sunning on the rocks down below. whatever sirened blood-and-gore event there was went unobserved, at least by me.

stoney earth, clear light blue sky. strayed way too far up to Saint-Jean-de-Fos. for the lowness of the bridge i didn't see the road that forked away to Saint-Guilhem-le-Désert. asking for directions later crumpled my brain into a hard tinfoil ball... when i'm exhausted i can't speak, can't get the French words out or get them to make any sense at all! frustrating mouthful of wallpaper-paste...

up steep cobbled streets, through a mossy archway dripping with mountain water and around a corner - stone stairways, walls and patios merge into a flowerpot and hosta-cluttered courtyard before the gîte... and it's for sale!

probably with the detour i did 35K today and tomorrow is 37K. i'm taking an Aleve. these feet, man! i don't know. the moleskin rubbed off at some point and blisters formed behind the ankle. and surprise! damnable rot-craving flies at my sores like the bevy round a dégustation table. and there's that big toe... at least i now know there's some sort of blister beneath the nail. bubbly frog roe pus froths from the toe-tip when i press down on it... the weirdly ballooning-up nail turning the color of storm.

St-Guilhem-le-Désert was founded against this steep-sided ravine in the IXth Century with the opening of a monastery said to contain part of the 'True Cross.' it would be interesting to see how tall would tower the monolith made from all the 'True Cross' splinters put together one day, united from their diaspora. with the powerful Hérault River churning below, the monastery's mills made a wealthy production center of this canton and in the modern 'base de loisirs' sense it is still popular. 360 parking places for visitors, several white-water rafting / canoeing operations, local product venues... soap shops, jewelers, minerals, pottery, glass beads and blowers... that type of thing. a lot of venerable history occurred here but presently it exists as a face-lifted and newly furbished mercantile outpost in the hills. and without a grocery, bar, or tabac-presse i can't shake the feeling that St-Guilhem is just a medievally facaded shopping mall despite its 'One of the Prettiest Villages in France' designation. that's the feel i feel. and in a bizarre twist of relic-grubbing, the monastery's actual cloister is back in the New York Metropolitan Museum of Art's medieval architecture branch in Fort Tryon Park, Manhattan... overlooking the Hudson River! it got whisked away when this whole place was in rock pile ruins.

i did buy a stone from a jewelry shop - 'jaspe rouge' ...a marrow-colored chalcedony with qualities of enthusiasm (alegría!) and meditation... thought it was a beneficial combination. jaspe rouge 'renders the spirit lively, stimulates action and eloquence, reinforces the body's energy, fosters courage and enterprise, combats aging, eases bleeding, helps scaring, regulates the liver,' and several other things i'm not able to translate but which i assume are positive, or else who'd buy the polished rock?

fried garlic. added some cooked rice and milk leftovers in the fridge... added water, dried basil, and the instant soup packet which has to be from the Corte Inglés in Seville. a bang-up soup. will have the rest thickly as congee for petit déj in the morning.

genial older Dutch couple here... what is it in the Dutch spirit that emanates graciousness? roughly plotted out the coming night stays... eleven days straight to Toulouse if i choose not to pillow on a rest day.

8/23/2006

soft dawn rays
    hang peach bright
        light-berries
    on lacquer waxen boxwood leaves,
        adeste fideles in the mind.

8/23/2006

tart cranberry scent of wild boxwood
    and sun-warm rosemary spice,
quiet garrigue dappled light,
    light cricket massage,
        and the deep-blue-sky breeze
            comb whiskers and thighs ~
    i am walking
        again.

journal - 8/24/06

warm in the gîte but a night breeze blew in from the heights... fountain water plashing in the mossy stone pool a storey down below. the Dutch couple got up soon after i arose. reheated my porridge, had a breakfast bar and a bowl of tea chatting with them. they once did the GR 5 from Holland! Rotterdam to Santiago... that trail's topping my list.

a steep and switchbacking morning climb. from sparse-growth

crumbling stone cliffs on one side of the mountain to thick forests on the other, the comfy tree-huddled trail rose following the curve of ridge and outcropping.

Arboras. by the roadside, a 'France Télécom Bonjour' phonebooth... made the appropriate calls to reserve ahead at the upcoming gîtes. surprising me from the receiver, "May I help you?" she asks with British brushstrokes. stopped two women on their way to the car to question if there was a store or a bakery or an anything around? they generously offered to get me something from their pantry but said, "Non." nothing here! all residents drive so there's no need for the little neighborhood alimentaciones of rural Spain. and for that matter the French are so American in their self-containment they hardly feel the need to leave the house... no paseos, no evening constitutionals through the streets. Josefina once told me when she first arrived in the U.S. she wondered where all he people were. all those grand manicured and empty lawns... in the Spain of her youth if you had two blades of grass out front you put three chairs around them and hung out with the neighbors. but that was before the West went televised and catatonic.

left Arboras about 10:30H and got to Saint-Jean-de-la-Blaquière at 14H! what!? it was only 10K away! must have missed an exit off a switchback lacet somewhere and switchbacked well after where i should have. figured things out with map, sun, eye and mind, and headed out through the vine-rows and horse pens to what i thought was Usclas-du-Bosc... but, you're never ahead of the game! it was only the long circuitous way around to Saint-Jean.

the grocery, of course, was closed at this hour but i passed a temporary looking snack bar among a scattered flock of white plastic tables and chairs... the type of simple structure usually seen harlequined in carnival lights, though here it looks as if the carnival has moved on and left him alone in an empty parking lot. big fat cook plops a steaming rare burger and a wet omelet with fries in front of the regular beside me as soon as he sat down. two firemen chatting with a greybeard drinking panachés... frizzy blond-headed toddler screaming blood not getting what he wants. glad i stopped and ate despite the wee banshee's tantrum.

tidal wave crashing winds battered on and off all day depending on the angle of mountain and front... lightly rained for a while... distant thunderclaps from across the rain-veiled plain.

proceeded on and up over hills and ridges, always walled-in by the green sound of pines whispering. realized at some point that the trail hadn't read the guide, so i left it in the pack and kept to the red-white striped GR waymarkings on stump and stone and somehow swung back well away from my destination to view a distant volcano-crater's lava dome surrounded by a lake. more vocal horses... already ate my last apple. désolé cheval.

i swear back by the priory a waymarker said 4.5K to Lodève. three hours later! i rang at the gîte after nearly passing Lodève entirely. saw the town miniaturely below and knew i had to descend one way or another. ended up stomping straight down the mountainside through private vineyards, backyards, lawns, and over shapely hedgerows... butt-sliding down scree to the river bridge.

before finding the gîte... a fruit and veg stand. got two nectarines that burst in my mouth like a milk carton in a Rottweiler's jaws. nectar-wet-handed i bought two more.

the night's lodging is in a B & B run by an ex-pat British couple and i have a cozy corner room here. their deck, sunroom and gardens look out over the slate-roofed center - a center dominated by the powerfully buttressed and square-towered Cathédrale de Saint Fulcran... mountainous cloud banks beyond. i shouldn't afford to stay another day but this is not my style. i want to get a feel for the places i'm passing through. one facelifted village skipped - ok. but two in a row? no. by the time ablutions were over it was 19H and to have two mere hours of chilly daylight left and a bolt out early tomorrow... no. not my style. it's got be more than just getting there.

found this Vietnamese restaurant and thought, why not? husband and wife wear all the hats so service is sloooow. their 'cocktail maison' is a rosé sweetened with lychee juice and a lychee fruit garnish. crackling spring rolls and a bun nem nuong. candy colored plastic lantern strings tassel the terrace canopy.

8/24/2006

last night's leftover stew for breakfast
    and bowl of tea in the belly warm,
  a bootstep on shattered shale
      trail walking song.
canyon climbing, canyon billiard ball
    pocketing the rising sun rays,
  dusty orange, rose, and
      silver-grey-weathered-wooden-fence hues...
these morning sky colors cataract down
    ragged cliffs
  to one whispering tree-hid stream westwarding
      below mountainside switchbacks ~
the wind through eroded gorge faces plays
    organ and oboe reeds,
  plays drum brush brushing oaks,
      and the harmonizing chorus trues
    climbing to crescendo heights
i, one boxwood, and one coloratura jubilant tor-clung pine.

8/24/2006

scotch pine muffled,
  the winding red-dirt mountain trail rises...
graze and agro-patchwork plains below ~
    distant grey virga rain cone veils, thunder rolls,
  a storm-shroud brooding goddess paces eastwardly away.

*

while walking west i wonder
    how to keep lightsome high wind sounds
        fresh in my ears
            from village to town...
    the cacophony rattling mind.

8/24/2006

    sun breaks,
        mountain greys with
  rain veils on the way ~
stopped asking why broken-in boots still
    blister and erode heel flesh
        to redden sink water
            washing socks.
may tomorrow's trail
    open as many inner eyes
        as morning does outside.

8/24/3006

    soft bed
        thick sheets
  nape nestling pillow
        and a door to close
      napping
          while rain falls.

journal - 8/25/06

so stayed i did.

after a fruit, boiled egg and cold cut petit déj i went to the Cathedral for a sit. organist practicing on the time-weathered and rodent-worn instrument whose keys and stops 'tock' with each wind-changed note... water drops in deep well sounds. narrow and golden stained-glass windows concave out behind the altar in the airy Gothic apse. storm-front cloud boulders rolling by outside. softly pulsing upon my lap, the honey light entrances, exploring hues. out back - an incidental cloister, unadorned grey stone arcades, a boxwood hedge, a twisted olive tree and pine.

le Musée Fleury was highlighting Berthe Morisot - sister-in-law to Manet. enjoyed her progression from thick bold lines to smooth faces. enjoyed the Fauvist, Raoul Dufy - his 'champs de blé,' 'la citrouille,' 'jardin de plantes,' 'grand orchestre,' colorfully shirted jockeys on the shimmering green background... the geometric fragmentation of birds in flight over Côte d'Azur white marina buildings. could have spent more time in the Fleury but with the rain it was becoming packed with people and hot for a museum.

back at the B & B i got a handcrafted waxen seal of a warbling bird for a tampon. cool. the Brits are artists and i won't be showing them my scratchings. he's got the habit of perfecting the features of one face on the canvas, so the same leather-wizened cheeks and sparkling eyes look down from the frames in the garb and trappings of farmer, sailor, thief, and lord.

French dogs love feet! that dog in the Saint-Gilles-du-Gard tabac-presse, and here - Sally's dogs are at her feet too, lapping like mad. she tells me the Dutchies showed up sopping wet and, poor things, they had the same addition of 10K problem as i did after the priory. saw them on the street later and directed them to a prepared food shop where i had stocked up earlier. my backpack is going to be heavy with prunes and nuts but if skies are overcast i can do without carrying water. if i get thirsty i'll osmose.

went back to the Vietnamese restaurant for another refreshing cocktail maison and fried prawns with sauced vegetables sizzling on an iron platter. there must be an international company that makes Asian / American Muzak. i'm hearing a 'you don't have to say you love me just be close at hand' instrumental with Asian strings... just like back at the old Saigon Restaurant in Allston, which i swear played Bryan Adams' 'Summer of '69' in that style while i savored hot and sour Fisherman's Soup with pineapple, sprouts, tomato, shrimp and salmon! ...the faces are often vague but i remember the meal. their daughter is still amusing herself quietly with imagination, ribbons and dolls... 'lah da da dah-life goes on.'

Friday, August 25th, 2006.
Subject: I met the 'Fool on the Hill'

...and he's British!
Bushwhacking through dense garrigue undergrowth and around deep gully erosion's labyrinthine ways... a you-call-that-a-trail!? leads steeply up to Usclas-du-Bosc, and seated on a sunny stone bench there I met the Fool on the Hill who pointed me the way through the narrow streets. I could tell he was a Brit by their common habit of grammatical precision without the faintest attempt at an accent.

90 years old and lonely in his age, he was an aviator in WWII... missed death eight times flying missions... maybe slight dementia in his red-rimmed eyes. He owned an antique shop in the center of London for many years... sold it for 8000L and bought a small hamlet not far from here. He sold that years later for 60,000L and bought this modest house in Usclas. Says he likes to laugh and sing, and he started humming Piaf... "Sur la route, la grande route un jeune homme va chantant..." I sat with him for a while on the sunny stone bench, conversing, looking out over the green valleys, blue mountains and patchwork plains beyond him, all the things he's soon to become. "Une fille pleurait... la da dahh da-dum..."

About a week ago I set out from Arles and headed into the wind-lashed marshlands and reed beds of the Camargue, egrets flashing white wings, bone-grey horses rolling on their backs scratching spines, heavy hooves swiping arcs across the blue Midi skies... then left it all quickly behind. Even on foot the French landscape changes like a rabid man's mind. There's a poem by Langston Hughes where the poet has God in the midst of creation crying out "BRING FORTH! BRING FORTH!!" ...and crossing a borderline river, Languedoc brings it on: wild olives shimmer, black on the branch figs so ripe the fruit has burst open into four succulent flesh petals in offering to bird, bat, bee and sweet-toothed fly... smooth green almond fruit casings cracked apart with summer-baked nuts within... hillside nectarine orchards spread out over grapevines dangling tight fruit clusters and then, like Keystone Kops driving, o mercy I hit a wall.

I hit a wall or the Chemin rodeo-roan bucked me high and I struck the ground hard. Stopped in Montpelier for several days. Was it me trying to impose the Vía de la Plata upon the Chemin d'Arles? The usual suspects lurking luminate in the shadows... fear, fearitation, wanting things to be different than they are... "It's not the long road ahead that wears you out; but the grain of sand in your shoe," is the Arabian saying - or those euphemized grains in the mind. I mention this as another aspect of the trail... something I haven't mentioned since a few rantings back in Spain, but the 'Way' is more than an earthen trail. It is a knowing leviathanic beast that can crush as well as caress... the sea when a mariner raises southern-cut sails on northern waters. Just watch the canvas shreds vanish in slowly widening wake lines.

Taking a rest day in the city of Lodève to focus... Lodève, from the Latin - 'lutum' ...a malleable clay, praised for its use in adobe and kitchen pottery, has been quarried at the confluence of these two rivers since 45 B.C. when Nero established a colony here. In the XVIIIth Century it was home to one of only two royal manufactories of carpets and tapestries... and in the XXth Century it was the center of fierce resistance against the Nazis. It's not my intention to sound like a freshman history reader but I hike all day through the mountains and arrive in a simple, attractive town and the ground I tread upon is studded with time's jewels.

A few days here in Lodève and hopefully, with a spirit re-aligned, I head into the inland Mediterranean mountains whose white limestone cliffs, by the magic of erosion, sedimentation and mineral seepage are somehow lit... yes, glowingly lit, lucent and illumined in pure golds, roses, greys, and streaked with sparse forest green... then higher into imposing 850... 970...1120 meter heights of les Montagnes Noires.

  Jim

 may we have ease of mind;
  may we have comfort of heart;
   may out lives be peaceful lives.
    ~the buddha

journal - 8/26/06

dark clouds closing in from the north blocked the sun so i waited until 7H to leave. the trail rose steeply up the hill behind the B & B... eyrie neighborhood roads winding around scattered eyrie perched homes, then into the wooded hills. so resplendent a rainbow above. there is something rudimentary about a window prism's refracted light fanned against a wall... something consummate in a rainbow-scarred stormy sky. a magical thing the clouds soon swallowed. then the mists began. northern thrown mists that never amounted to actual rain but which made the day raw-grey. and the trail, after essing among bracken, blackberry and bramble snarled mountain tops, turned face-on into the wind howling 'Danse Macabre' haunted reed and windwood orchestrations... the gale through these bracken, blackberry twig and bramble vine voices harmonizing scordatura discord in their utter plenitude. switchbacking, switchbacking, switchbacking up...

came upon two dogs on the grassy wood road... one gutturally growling. got ready rooting my feet to the mountain with balance, chi and staff, but no need. they were friendly and funny animals! could tell they've been together for a long time... got the feel they're vagabond strays... named them Eeyor and Scamp. Scamp, and his excited non-stop wiggly butt and tail, would not let ANY attention be given to Eeyor. any hand held out was licked lavishly by Scamp and he'd muzzle-nuzzle his way in between Eeyor and i with puppy-like selfish glee, nip Eeyor, and Eeyor in donkey-Eeyor's voice would look at me from a short distance and say with sad but understanding eyes when i tried to pet him... 'IIIII knowww, doonnn't bother - he's just going to bite me on the chinnnnn.' i tried anyway. they followed, then lead.

following the inner crux between lowland-reaching slopes...

BANG!!!ZZZZZZZZZZZZZZZZZZZZZZZZZZII
IIIIIIIIIIIIUUUUUUUUUUUUUUUUUUUBA
NG!!!ZZZZZZZZZZZZZZZZZZZZZZZZIIIIIIIII
IIIIIUUUUUUUUUBANG!!!ZZZZZZZZZZZIII
IIIIIIIIIIIIUUUUUUUUUUUUUUUU...

never heard bullets whizzing through the air like that before, strangely slow. hunters down in the valley... hunters on the wood road above. first one makes a quiet sign with index and lips and i'm thinking - yeah, a dead man is pretty fucking quiet. then nearing one of their jeeps, a handwritten sign in the windshield... Chasse au Sanglier! Chasse au Are You Kidding Me?! if there are wild boar running around here like hell i'm being quiet. they're gonna hear me coming. i read <u>Old Yeller</u>.

put my jacket on backwards to avoid a sweaty backpacked back and felt more comfortable wind-breaker-breast-plated against the blowing mist and raw.

as all company eventually does, the dogs became a bother. they were not intelligent creatures. when the trail followed the Departmental for a while they would not get out of the way of coming cars. they'd even run towards the car head-on as it barreled down at them. i was incredulous. got many driver-side dirty looks and annoyed head shakings... they're not mine pal! even had the fantasm of one of them, probably Scamp, getting whacked by a car. wounded, i'd have to kill him to end the suffering... how would i get the blindfold over his eyes? my mind put a firing squad cigaret in his mouth and i wondered who would find his broken skull-crushed body with a blindfold and a rain-soaked Gauloise?

stepping into Bernagues they found a friend to ass-sniff and frolic with and vanished in the boxwood shrubs.

after Bernagues, a switchbacked descent into a verdant valley, like a waterless fyord... and tucked in the deep inner curve of the valley - a house, a mansion, a medieval hunting Manse. what solitude. to stand on that front porch and look outward with these green mountains shawling a comfort wrap around... imagine the night sky gazing! the trail longed the other side of the valley, up and over and across train tracks into the shimmering jewel of Joncels, and i found the warmest welcome - un accueil chaleureux!

the 'gîte' is in a small stone inn which was bustling with the lunch crowd when i arrived. the proprietor is the maitre d' and dishwasher. his proprietress wife is a Lithuanian powerhouse whose elderly dad carves all these sculptures out of local chestnut wood and boxwood wood... crazed Eastern European ogres, howling beast and folk tale faces anthropomorphically emerging from rough logs, lying on stones, hanging off interior walls and chevron-beamed ceilings. out front, the ivy-veined stonewall herds their gardens around the pool... gardens of roses, buddleia, sage, the only oleander i've seen that's yellow, coreopsis, indian blanket, ornamental grass, small cypresses, palm, asparagus fern, echinacea, petunia, dianthus and datura.

the owners don't want pilgrims to wash clothes in the sink so they launder for us. 'The machines are running for sheets and towels anyway. What's a few more clothes?' she says with a fatalist's purse pouted lips and a shrug to the equally indifferent sky.

Joncels is built in bastide style - the residences' side-by-side back walls forming the fortifications around the center and around the

Benedictine Abbey stronghold which now offers its once cloister as an arcaded marketplace. the majority of buildings are in unlivable ruin, but the hamlet is experiencing a slow resurgence of life. heard a few Brit voices from over overgrown garden walls and there were more in the dining room when i came in. they love it down here.

coming in on the Chemin it is hard to say whether a place is isolated or not. there could easily be an autoroute or an urban center nearby, but who'd know? the full to bursting lunch crowd had to have come from somewhere!

Jean-Pierre is the other pilgrim here.

8/26/2006
wind-mist lashed mountain heights...
    desiring anywhere-else escape.
  fiery yellow, russet, and pale green
      dying fern berms line a volcanic black ashy
        trail turning
      down into chestnut tree bough shelter,
    down from the harshening sky ~
      trail dogs cock their heads
wondering why i've stopped
      to listen to winds which
        no longer strike me.

8/26/2006

eastern gold cloud-mountain flames,
    steep switchbacked forest hike
        to heights once miracle-covenant arced,
            now storm front swallows the rainbowed sky...
        distance is grey and near.
    tree-toppling gales blast the heights
        and i wonder what firesmoke
            teas steam below.

journal - 8/27/06

got up early. Giedre was downstairs and chatty in an embracive way. the table was set out with fig jam, breads, cheese, teas and coffee. hoped to like, but didn't care for the rosemary jelly. they bought this place 25 years ago in roofless ruins and have slowly rebuilt it up. decided to make it a tool to pay its continuing growth so they added a restaurant... added rooms when time and finances allowed. told her my perception of how coming in on the trail Joncels seemed isolated but "Mais non!" was her retort. 45 minutes to Montpelier! two hours to Italy! two hours to Spain! three to Barcelona! the beauty of these places embraced in a green interlace of mountains... the feel of being far removed... the tight nestle of nature all around. then in a quick hop, skip and a drive... culture and cultures!

left about 7H. a tranquil wooded trail, then - quiet! among the thick trees, the leaf-swathed sky... boar-scraped black loam patches.

Lunas... mellow Sunday morning river sounding through the gold sunrayed village in a verdant mountain bowl. salt-and-pepper flecked granite homes with lichen stained terra cotta roof tiles, the stone church tower focals a center in the lens's eye.

another easy trail to Le Bousquet-d'Orb - Église Saint Martin towering high against an abrupt mountainside overlooks the granite town below. a horn blares, husky black poodle mutt comes barreling down the road running away. is that dissonance really necessary at this peaceful morning hour? further up ahead the white van making bread deliveries to the neighborhoods blares again. she opens the hatchback and i find me waiting behind three women in slippers and housecoats... "Pâtisseries?" i ask... yeah, baby! eating a myrtilles and custard tartelette in the shadow of the stone church is better than any bloody eucharist. white-haired woman hanging clothes outside on a line... and with her wet hands steaming in attestation we concur on the cold. dad pushing son in a red plastic kiddie car. their dog charges me protecting her ward and dad starts yelling, flailing angry arms like he's thwarting bees and bats making me and his wife laugh loudly, but i'm glad it obeyed. vicious Dachshund bitch. beady-eyed white geese periscope over a hedge, inspecting the ruckus.

and i started the long steep cloud-ward climb. first hunter! second hunter! third... fourth fifth sixth seventh! all posted where the trail leveled in the inner swing between mountain spurs. a cyclist with bike a-shoulder coming toward me... told him it looked like East Germany back there and we laughed. first hunter asked if i was THE American. he said Jean-Pierre passed by 15 minutes before. somehow he got ahead of me. the last hunter said J-P looked nervous, commenting on the speed of his passage... more mountain laughter, but no, that's his frenetic pace.

under-limb and under-leaf tunneling, tunneling, tunneling through high mountains today... 900 meters! chilled. cliff and mountain-face channeled winds syphon the warmth from my pores. sat early for a snack-break... bonjour tomate. "on n'est pas riche mais on vie bien," reminding happiness is no trick of 'the other' but emanates only from within. ate tomato, apple, nuts, and prunes... pffft... au revoir noyau. reached for my jaspe rouge but it was gone. picked up a pretty mica-glinted stone reminding self the learning continues and you never really know... "Are you sure?" Thich Nhat Hanh encouraging a sangha to write down and frequently read... "Are you sure?" am i sure? is my perception pearl or hardened pus?

way up, closer to 'God' it was goddamned cold and windy. inspiring views around of mountains flush with beech, chestnut and oak. whole mountainsides of replanted conifer rows with interspersed rows of seeping post-harvest stumps incensing the air with spicy resin. what a wonder to have this trail as a resource living nearby... to recharge the soul with the sound of alpine winds thick in the ears.

Col des Clares (590M). Col de Peyremale (681M). Col du Liourel (702M). Col des Serviès (893M). le Mont Cabanes (902M). Col de Layrac (765M). Col de las Couches (409M).

the last leg down into Saint-Gervais-sur-Mare was narrowly brush and bramble lined. telephoned Paola from the 'France Télécom Bonjour' phonebooth and met her on the sycamore pillared square. she led me to the municipal gîte where J-P's already settled in.

the bakery is open. bought a loaf full of roasted chestnut chunks and prunes - heavy, delicious, satiating. if the Holy Host had half that meed i might take up kneeling. bought a slab of pizza and two quiche-lettes for later.

crowned with a walled and cypress-spired cemetery, Saint-Gervais has its back tucked up against a cliff-face. protectively hunkered between mountain and the river, it is another harbor for those seeking hiking / biking / kayaking pleasures deep in the heart of le parc régional de Haut-Languedoc. but the season is late and seekers are few. between car door and chassis a man morphs black wet-suit, white ass, dun dry clothes phases and drives a bungeed rooftop kayak away...

8/27/2006

        mountain trail serpentines,
   black-back beetle shines the
     green wallow
between worn white gravel tracks ~
katabatic blasting winds knock
     me backwards on my ass writing lines...
   laughing loud with no-one around
      fills my soul fuller
        than repose.

journal - 8/28/06

J-P was up and out first. i closed up the gîte and clinked key through the locked mailbox slot.

a narrow road with girthly 20-foot high stonewalls leads out of Saint-Gervais... out and so soon into phantasmically haunted chestnut forests. their tight trunk clumps and gnarly knots, boles, and limbs in the shifting light and fog need spare whittling skill to evoke the weird creatures of the mind into being. in a cutting J-P saw a sanglier!

descent into Andabre... a stream-side community in the woods with titanic mountain spines enveloped in mist behind. someone kept a red-painted pen of rabbits who thumped nervously at my passing... watching me with their aghast black side-eyes.

following the stream, dense pine forests darken the way to Castanet-le-Haut. so thankful to have this time to be enchanted by the movement of water around rocks. passed by a few rural well-kempt homes and grounds... a woman hosing her across-the-lane garden from an upper patio stops the arcing shower to let me pass and smirks in a way i know the sulfurous imp within wants to spray me.

on the switchbacking climb i missed a turn with my 'out of the wind' head held down behind the hat brim and digressed far awry. sat on a stump for another "on n'est pas riche mais" i'll celebrate anyway pilgrim's lunch of the dense chestnut and prune bread, tomato, raisins, cheese, peanuts ground to meal between my teeth under pine shelter and passing mist falls... a suite of white braided breaths rising, stone altar, bark paten, the chalice of cupped palm and stream wine. this third day in the mountains - so soothing, wrapped in a wanderer's cloud cowl.

solitary eagles' eyrie house all closed up - une maison piègée... a booby-trapped house. on the back side, propped on a picket, a carved face like a slain Orc or Cangeceiro head in warning. stay away!

kept on climbing through all ages of planted pine broken by expanses of beech-wind song... could see the low plains pulsing light and shadow beneath the advancing clouds. down down down longly into Murat-sur-Vèbre... geraniums line the lane's high wall, goat-shit pebbles and sour-cider-scented wild apple windfalls.

Murat-sur-Vèbre is still at 800M... misty grey. the gîte privée is a former convent, once in ruins, but presently converted into B & B guest-rooms above and the bunked dormitory below. off the kitchen, chiseled out of the limestone bedrock is a low stone seclusion alcove the nuns used, now rustically kept with a writing desk and lamp. upon waking from a deep nap the gîte was raw and cold. i don't think that's uncommon in light of the stacks of blankets available.

came up to the center. not much. this isn't even a real bar but the hotel's vacant dining room bar they're letting me sit in with my afternoon sippers to write for a while. quiet. weird. people in this region have taken to screwing overlapping slabs of black slate to the windward / stormward side of their granite homes, giving a scaled carapace look to the brood huddled villages.

called the Office de Tourisme in la-Salvetat-sur-Agout to hold a bed for me. bought garlic, onion, and canned lentils and will stir in a pre-fab grated carrot salad with mustard vinaigrette... o holy stew steaming in the raw late-August mountain night. J-P ate an entire two pound can of 'dauphinoise' - basically scalloped potatoes with garlic and cream. that's it! ever hear of nutrition? sustenance is not just what fills you. i offered, but he didn't think the carrot would go well with the lentils. what? why would any vegetable not go well with any legume or grain? what the? if nothing else, learn to bite thy tongue in time.

8/28/2006

    raw grey afternoon,
purple heather inflects the trail,
    wind in high mountain pines,
        mist and cloud-fog forms reflecting
            the flow of phantasms behind pupil and mind ~
    all i need is a burner and
        a pot in the low valley abode
            to make a marvel
                of a tea-bag.

8/28/2006

10,000 branches wash
    one high mountain wind,
        steep slope-side dirt road winding
            round alpine spurs, empty
    but for my walking here
and the resinous wet-spice scent of hewn pine ~
        picking up
            a quiet stone
                stills the spinning mind.

8/28/2006

wild wind-wave crashed
    mountain songs seething
        beech, oak, and pine leaf refrains
all sift my mind back to Now.
    mountainside silence is visibly still.
across the gorge, another valley slope roars
    Nature's laughter.

8/28/2006

eastern black mountain, dawn cloud-brims flame ~
    light rises round
        a weathered-grey
            rotting stump
        ringed in purple heather sparking
the boar-hoof torn trail.

8/28/2006

    between sunbright stonewall and
wind-whispering grapevines,
following a copper-colored trail to
    its vanish in a wild fig grove,
        the little mind telling
        long stories
under light blue arcing skies ~
        grasshopper thumps my calf
to launch silly circles
    in October-chilly
        August air.

8/28/2006

    dense chestnut forest.
under broad serrate leaves and overcast sky
        the night yet holds bold shadowed sway.
       crickets gently ripple eveningly ~
   fierce fiend and fellow faces
in bark twisted limbs and boles ~
     dogs give bay to boar-scent
        upon the other mountain's slope.
       between prey and prayer
         slips the knife.

journal - 8/29/06

a day of slow descents. a wooded trail. not much vista for the ensconsement of trees... tunneling, tunneling, a mole in the mind tunneling. Black Elk's "everything sacred moves in a circle," circling to the center of all things.

on a pine needle matted wood-road, two people further up ahead mushroom hunting... a white-black brinded dog running silently, rooting out something from the humus then bounding away. saw him much later sitting in a field, head tilted, eyes cast high, transfixed by the voice of his master's sky. met another shaggy Spaniel by the Villelongue church. so happy he was to be scratched with articulate fingers and not his own claws. a diminutive pastoral church among trees with an attached Presbytery-shanty and graveyard grounds walled around. writing a note in their low-tabled ledger, a stone archway gives frame to simply overlooking blue lake, green forested hill horizon, and thick racing clouds above. from the shadows an old man kneeling waves, and rasps "Que Dieu te garde." then goes back to his beads.

a change from the mountain heights... from goat-shit on the transhumance trails to golden brown cattle casting shadows in low-rolling fields. from an arm's length away i could have watched that cable-muscled steer chaw for a very long time. there is such conscious presence in the brawny beast, such awareness that, fearlessness that he could crush me by merely thinking of his hoof... but the OT hours kept me moving on.

booked it to get to la-Salvetat-sur-Agout before 13H when the OT closes. made it and J-P is here! thought he was doing a double étape today but apparently the gîte in Anglès is closed... something unpleasant about sewage and pipes.

la-Salvetat is a larger village than most, these past several days. as the name suggests, it, and many of these mountain towns from isolation and proximity to Spain, were founded as a 'sauveté' ...a bastion of safety, a fortified commune tied to the authority and strength of the monastery or abbey capping the high-ground. a carbonated mineral spring from Antiquity has made this burg and its waters famous throughout France. built steep and close and spiraling up a limestone spur by the river, the concentric streets are tucked with grotto-like corners and caged songbird-echoed squares... haunts of ever sweeping mémés and napping cats.

the gîte is in a former Presbytery... time-and-foot smoothed stone steps, fortress thick walls, built like it was meant to do shouldered battle with the Devil himself. three simple cell-like, twin-bedded upper rooms. rooms have heaters and the damp, in shifting fog-mist-rain phases, is beginning to accompany the grey skies. might dry clothes there despite the posted request.

this chill October weather in August pulls the energy out of me like heat from a pie... makes me nap-tired. the body working for locomotion and working to keep the vital torso innards warm.

two girls here got scolded by the bullish bartendress for serving me a pastis. they're too young to be behind the bar. interesting to watch and hear... families or friends must be visiting as one girl speaks only French and the other only English, but they're far from silent. they talk to each other knowing the words are square blocks and round holes but through gesture and eye there is reciprocal understanding.

sat in the bar's front 'room,' a glassed-in-against-the-chill patio... and while listening to clacking billiards games i tried to draw the patio balustrade and streets down below... a poor translation between eye and hand. more black carapaced lauze-sided buildings... the rain and snow must drive ferocious here.

ate early. bed early. melancholy under chilling rain.

8/29/2006
morning meadow-side
    hidden in the trees trail,
  back-lit mountain ash
      berries cluster coals,
one wolf skull hung on a low branch,
    one white birch peels scrolls the wind unfurls.

journal - 8/30/06

funny all the things fret about never happen. all that mind rap about not having time now with the darkening days to draw and explore the environs... and there's not been much all week to occupy either intention.

wind slapped rain hard against the windows most of the night... so 'XVth Century' to be high up in an infrangible stone Presbytery listening to the buffet and storm. the new pèlerin was staying on another day. from his description i think he's wracked with tendonitis down between knee and ankle. Ivan.

cold this morning. i could see my breath at the start. threatening dark clouds never amounted to anything but shadows and fear. footsteps approaching from behind... J-P almost passed me but then realized he left his shaving kit back at the gîte - a gîte that's the first place we didn't have to drop the keys off in a locked box upon leaving, too.

today's trail... much the same. hilly, wooded, sometimes lined with ivy-wrapped pines. at one point, for the several days unbleached by the sun, an emerald green greenest meadow breasts a sloping break in the trees... blue mountains beyond.

got to Anglès early. about 11H. a small, local produce market going on on the unusually steep square anchored by two grocery stores and a closed café. there must be a lot of frequent Brit and Dutch campers somewhere nearby. saw both language's newspapers in the grocery. buying a Yop, an older lady at the cash register told me where the campground was after i asked about an open café. she questioned me about the trail... compassion emanating. at the hilltop pastry shop a pip-squeak kid, grunt-pushing hard, opens the door for me with satisfied smiles. bought a palmier for me and a tresse for him. drank my Yop and dumped the annoying pebbles that keep leaping into my boots out.

i think with all the mountains, hills, and passing fronts this region experiences frequent micro-bursts... many limbs and trees down in localized places.

got to Boissezon and the Mairie, (with the gîte key), is closed. called the posted number and got an answering machine that offered another number, but i had to call and re-call to hear it correctly... rapid talking and my French numbers aren't so well-practiced. as i'm calling a third time juggling paper, pen and ear-shouldered phone, J-P rounds the corner! i think he's a shape-shifter and runs stag-like through the woods because i never saw him after he went back to the gîte to get his shaving kit. he never passed me and yet here he is ahead. he did this once before... shape-shifters. he and '?' are in the small adjunct gîte beside the main. Chantale, a hospitalière with her own ring of keys and owner of the Deux Mousquetaires Restaurant, she was away until 18:30-19H so i showered up and laundered at J-P's place, then went exploring. the town follows the mutual bend of river and ridge but there's just nothing more there than residences and artist studios high up the bluff. Monday's Sunday silence. did 40K today and i am beat.

poking around the narrow neighborhood roads between cliffs high and low... man and son hauling downed limbs through the sharp clatter of street-crashed terra cotta roof tiles.

Chantale returned and smilingly set me up with tasty restaurant leftovers to reheat later... leftovers of baby squid, (encornets), stewed in tomato sauce with potatoes! and then she unlocked the main gîte for me. HUGE! out the backdoor is a backyard canyon of sorts and i am so envious. the hulking hillside rock-face and the three-storey gîte's back wall form an atrium with top-heavy corn plants, rubber trees, and rhododendrons growing down below... overlapping hard plastic sheets form the roof above. a lush grotto i'd spend much time in inhaling the sweet-rot scent of greenhouses i always crave in New England's February.

turned on the electric heater to dry my clothes. no way they'll dry in this temperature. and that first-of-the-day physical sensation of slipping on dawn's cold damp socks... obscene metaphors fill the mind.

journal - 8/31/06

slept not that well... kept waking up more tired than before. might have been a bit creeped out, too - alone in that empty place. the eerie grotto / atrium... dreamt of a vague murderer. not after me - just one out 'there.' arose at 6H. a breakfast of fruit, tea and toast. another frigid morning.

followed a musical stream up a narrow road... a wooded trail. laughably ferocious Lilliputian white dog and another one chained... barking brothers announcing my presence through the hamlet. October-crisp air in late August, scent of fallen apples and manure.

Castres is an engaging change from the people-sparse mountain villages... a small city with sunny stucco, stone and cross-beamed facades along the river running lively through it. a rest day tomorrow. wonder how that will change the faces on the Chemin? wonder who's behind? only about 13-14 étapes left until Spain.

glad to have two days here without much to do. i'm getting lost in 'doing' as patterns harden into habit, then rut. wondering if the Chemin is actually 'dry' or if i've been at it for so long? going to have to sit more. i remember a meditation teacher saying the other three positions are beneficial: recumbent, walking, and standing are all fine forms in which to practice, but you've got to sit. there's a miracle at the core of each experience but yagattasit! sounds like a Hindu saint. Sai Yagattasit says...

journal - 9/1/06

late night at the Irish pub with a rock-a-billy band rocking to level ouch. fun to watch the crazy-busy bartenders spinning the lazy-susan of syrups... banana, mango, peach, almond, cassis, mint, grenadine... name it - for beer and beer cocktails! only had one draft but they gave it fifty flavors.

checked out the Goya museum. Picasso's self-portrait and 'Bust of a writing man' ...amazing. a flamenco guitarist and singer painted by Carlos Pradal evoking motion and heat. Goya's four series of engravings - insane! the Caprices - the Disasters of War - Tauromanchie - the Proverbs. the guy was wacked. the Tauromanchie was straight forward, but the others... he must have had himself some hellish night-terrors. bought a 'there's so much to suck' postcard of ragged hags with vampire souls slurping fat and marrow out of infants' limbs. wondering if there's Goya wallpaper? though i'd probably have daylong nightmares. if people only knew, if people only knew - they'd never open that blue can of garbanzos.

five days from Lodève... through the Black Mountains... Toulouse is four days away.

9/1/2006

cold breath, brilliant morning,
    chill-thickening stream sounds...
        sun warms the stone village and cooling bed,
   another village far ahead

      *

hiking west a rising sun lobs rays over the mountain behind me
     and
        goldens today's distance beyond...
    traipsing the vale through mountain shade
        black hole crows croak for silent stones

      *

needle-rot russet trail winds
   through ancient-leaved fern
      miming ancient-leaved pine
        in prehistoric pre-word
          wind song ~
  spore, cone, mind...
     walking here,
    breathing white cloud sky.

9/1/2006

ONE
    sweet-toothed
        blackberry feasting beastie
        leaves seed speckled
            shit ringlets upon
            the meadow winding trail.

9/1/2006

the morning forest steams cauldronly
        releasing yesterday's inhaled warmth ~
chilled horses' chortled neighs...
        volplaning hawks' jubilant peals pierce a clouded sky...
approaching th' approaching shadow-cast fringe
    between coming clouds and this sunny hill,
        last night's rain
            falls again...
the front-driven wind shaken trees.

9/1/2006

silence rings in the ears
        mooning through rain-darkened pine trunk lines
           and needle whispered shelter ~
                rhythmic bird calls coupled with rhythmic
            bird responses,
        one wild apple tree's
      cider-musky shade,
footsteps falling on the trail...

journal - 9/2/06

Saturday September Second - was it only one week ago i got shot at on a mountainside?

went to the morning window - a deep overcast shadow after two halcyon days of blue. a colorfully tented market going on on Castres' Place Jean Jaurès... they've powered down the gushing fountain-jets sodden toddlers usually run screaming through while their mothers sip and visit in café umbrella shade.

a deep overcast shadow from above after two halcyon days of blue, but as if in recompense... a supportive day. "Bon courage!" from a man on the bridge, horns beep on the road, hand waves from a tractor, a local whose house is down by the river bade me well... said the Chemin brushes by his back-porch. my kind of day all around... my kind of trail. those mountainous days experiencing nothing but the inside of woods and mind, broken by quiet stone enclaves whose denizens already seem to be in the early glaze of mountain hibernation... suffice it to say - i'm enjoying the change.

to walk out again even after only one day of rest is so... animative. wound out through neighborhoods, train tracks, river, rolling meadows, movement from agriculture to husbandry. couple donkeys come over to be scratched. came upon the most curious black and white brindeds i've ever seen. several came trotting well across the field to ogle me closely... others lumbered slowly, but i had an audience of at least a dozen bovines by the time i left them. lots of scrappy loud dogs. one woman apologized for her tirading hound. that my mere presence causes chaos makes me grin. kick a ripple in the Tao. most of the day followed a low mountain chain to the south, also heading west with me. for the croplands and private lands there is excessive zigzagging around properties.

stepped into Viviers-lès-Montagnes - a tabac-presse-grocery. got a strawberry Yop and an oreillette! ...translation to the eye, 'little ear' ...translation to the tongue, sugared little fried dough sheets and the dough is scented with dried peppermint leaves!

this area is scattered with 'communes.' four to five building clusters of farms and residences. stopped in one commune to un-pebble boots... two smiling chubby cherub siblings - the nude one on the trike i half expected to take wing.

the sun's not rising higher than 65 horizon degrees and an autumnal feel is spreading.

Adam in Autumn dangling... Adam in Autumn dangling... a fruit-laden, but leaf-bare, fig tree.

reiterating how i enjoy the change from the mountains today - gently undulant landscapes, mellow golden light, passing through flowered and cared for communes.

tourist offices around here hold the gîte key more often than the Mairie or agèd widows with nowhere else to go, so i bore strongly on before it closed midday... legs aching - those peanuts weigh in the pack. entered Revel, picked up a key at the OT and found the souped-up municipal gîte...

'halle' is the term used for a roofed open-sided marketplace quite common in this region. Revel's tiled, towered and clock cupola-ed 'halle' shades the center of the main square surrounded by arcaded shops and bars... kids on scooters being young and loud. a green grocer defines cornucopia with his toppling baskets - 3E for a bagful! and not knowing what Montferrand will be like on a Sunday i bought extra veg for tomorrow night.

went back to the gîte after drawing les Halles and Clarisse was waiting for me. as a member of the local Association de Saint Jacques de Compostelle, this is her week's stint to be the hospitalière here. she made an apple compote and plated figs from her tree. gracious woman, a retired secretary. she's done the Chemin from le-Puy in stages but wants to do Spain all in one swoop... has designs to establish a gîte in Gimont. i had to fight her to do my own dishes even though i made most of the mess with another garbanzo, tuna, tomato, and couscous stew. there was extra-virgin olive oil to pre-simmer and post-shine, and crunchy salt to garnish.

sweet baby Jesus i love my stews... powering heart and thighs over plains and mountain ranges.

journal - 9/3/06

the Canal du Midi starts after Montferrand but today's étape followed the narrow Rigole canal that feeds it. a moment standing in the shade... Claude stopped to talk. 67. spent five years in Australia as a diver-fisherman, (thus the quirky French / Aussie accent), and he worked for French Customs Coast Guard as diver-translator. he cycled out to the lake then on the way back stopped to pace along with me a while. talked about the Canal... amazing! ok, not the pyramids, but still... the mind behind it conceived 240K of canals for irrigation, transportation of freight, and to avoid North Africa's pirate-haunted Barbary Coast... flowing via raised beds over rivers, over train tracks, and over roads... 400 years ago!

around the recreational man-made lake fit for little more than carp and paddleboats, an extensive flea market festively unbound... umbrellas, canopies, junk and treasure. the restaurant with a droopy-eyed hound thinking it his duty to be the threshold... stopped there to enjoy a café crème and a croissant packed with almond paste. youngster looking at my pack, tall as him. had fun cajoling him to lift it. pods of cyclists taking breaks.

scratched on the café's bathroom wall is this lovely ditty:

> Quand vous rentrez dans ce lieu respectable
> Tenez-vous aussi bien qu'à table.
> Que les bords de cette cuvette
> Soient aussi nets que ceux de votre assiette,
> Car c'est ici que tombent en ruins
> Tous les trésors de la cuisine.

and quoting the Franco-American extended family of my childhood who tried to translate for my Dad, smiling politely, when they'd tell a joke and all burst out laughing... "It just isn't funny in English." and leave it at that.

took the 'Variante' away from la Rigole to cut some time off to Montferrand... out through hot fields, through a couple dusty dry communes...

the gîte in Montferrand is a fixed-up clutter of fortress-y former waterworks mill buildings radiating golden stone warmth... rill-trickling gardens on the other side of the gate. no one here when i arrived but the dorm being unlocked i settled in among the refurbished walls and close side-by-side bunks. the owner, a Brit with French wife, he wasn't so friendly at first. i think he thought i was a snooper ignoring the posted sign and checking out the property as i was all washed up, flip-flopped and daypack wearing when they came driving up the drive.

today was pure poetry... from days of mental discord in the orchards and vines... to days of physical difficulty in the mountains... to days of blindness in the forested hills seeing only the inner undersides of trees... to the communes and September light lit fields, poplars slowly losing their lode of leaves and the autumnal scent of tannic leaf-rot... to these days now following the Canal, trail and man heading westward to the sea under arching tree canopies. couldn't stop striding today. didn't resist. the bloody raw right heel...

i'll ignore the Chemin for two days and follow the Canal... so simple a trail i can leave in the dark.

journal - 9/4/06

woke uncertainly several times in universal darkness... are my eyes open or closed? toilets are in the far end of a non-adjoining building and the front-yard motion sensor light that clicked on at my motion hardly emanated into the absorbent pitch black.

left at 6:30H. sycamore canopies arching under an inky pre-dawn sky.

an all-tar path followed the autoroute closely for half the day. 'traffic' ratcheting within and without. 'not the way i want things to be' mind slapping 'peace in the present moment' mind around. between highway and Canal a field of cannabis opened up... resinous incense on the hot baked breeze and all manner of adverbial questions arising.

the obelisk back in Montferrand honors the Canal's architect, Pierre-Paul Riquet, and marks its highest point at 182M. now, heading toward Toulouse, the Canal keeps descending altitude, and beside the wet wooden froth-churned sluice gates there are signposts signaling the meters until the next lock giving an uneven cadence to the day. been in 'St Francis and the Sow' mind - remembering a thing its beauty and the thing responds in shines, smiles, shadows, and sighs. thanks Galway, for those lines.

i think i'm finally learning... this Chemin is 'lutin' - an imp, (on the wicked side), that'd never scorch the soul but it'll bite your brisket if you aren't watching. what Sparks said rankled my mind... that the woman who runs the gîte in Baziège is away on vacation and the local priest isn't that agreeable because he's obligated to give 'acceuil' and shelter to the pilgrims. a lot of internal noise about just continuing on to Toulouse and skipping all things problematic. and the guide says the trail is more interesting than the Canal.

arrived in Baziège about 12:30H but the Presbytery wasn't receiving until 14H. napped in the pigeon coo-ed park. inner fatigue from wishy-washy back and forthing, stay or continue on to Toulouse in one sweep, stay or continue on to Toulouse. wigwagging seesawing shuttlecocking brain energy is energy expended and will wear one down just as well as labor.

there are two Sundays in France, at least in the summertime. Sunday and Monday! who knew? all commerce in this one-main-strip town is closed up tight. no bar / café... church is locked. i don't want to sound like a 24 / 7 New Yorker but how does your business survive being only open to the public 30 hours a week? France isn't cheap. they tax the steps you take across the street. how does your business survive?

Priest doesn't trust the new pèlerin who came by. says he's a 'professional' and told me to watch my stuff. i don't know what he means by 'professional' but i do know this guy is irritatingly chatty. he's Spanish and goes right on jabbering his repetitive themes regardless the comprehension of his audience.

the automatic metal hangar door we're supposed to bang the Big Red Button and keep closed, but which everyone else leaves open, opens to the Presbytery's oil-stained pavestone patio lined with cars and sycamores, and shelters the lanky occupant of a brokedown caravan doing odd jobs Priest finds for him. he has a money-colored mama cat with twin kittens and a papa's-genes white and tan one... the lot of them skittish. he uses a difficult accent. got thrown out of Paris? trouble with the law or those outside the law. easy and generous. when i mentioned the nothing to do - all closed up... he offered me his place to watch a movie. put in a bootlegged 'Sin City.' cool! that's one way to spend two hours. ladies and gentlemen, Elijah has left the Shire.

another pèlerin from Toulouse settled in later.

i don't know. maybe Antonio is a crook. then again - you never know. Sparks said Priest wasn't friendly. now Generous Movie Man is telling me he pastorally does anything for everyone - un type merveilleux! and for that he's out straight busy. how do you live with multiple sides to each situation constantly shifting in front of your eyes? probably by ever asking and never answering "Am I sure?" dwelling in the openness between finition.

Antonio just passed by commenting on how hot it was as if it were the first time and then rattled on in Spanish as if we were in Madrid. Marc and i went over our opposing itineraries, of where we stayed and how it was, exchanging pointers... then i went to 'mattress' on the kitchen floor.

9/4/2006

along La Rigole ~
    invisible cow lows ripple misty morning meadow light,
        wild hops spice the air.
  willingly the canal takes me with
        on strange dream segue
            drifts to the sea.

      *

wilt-headed sunflower fields'
    star-count of black seeds swelling, drying, priming...
  corn rows' yellow streaked leaves and stalks
      rattle scarecrow bowels
      and bird-dom in September nut and berry rapture
        awakens music in the stones.

      *

canal bend, green-ivied grass berm, willow fountain, trail.
  French farm dog bays, baies are berries
    buried in Hudson's whales.
  ears steeped in sounds of stepping,
    sheep bleats, rooster crows,
      duck kwonks, cow lows
    in child's language game
      rotations far a-field from home.

*

leaf-sifted Sunday light dapples a serenading canal.
    acacia, sycamore, pine, walnut, willow,
        linden and oak trunks
    pillar the over-arching foliage woven tapestry
        telling sacred brindle tales
            as Cathedral stained glass walls do...
    or simply a color and form wonder
        upon a rippling waterway,
            upon a trail of earth-clay,
        and my brow returning to the timeless brew.

    *

the mysteries that please us aren't questioned,
    the mysteries that bleed us we've torn the unplumbed cosmos
        asunder
           to fictate our Heavens and Hells ~
silly ole bare human mind.

    *

acorn thumps a grassy mound
        miming
    his stone-struck-pole enlightenment
        long ago...
just smiles now,
        not today.
        not today.
    a curious bee buzzes my ear
        and vanishes over shorn weathered-grey stubble fields.
shorn weathered-grey stubble fields rolling away with
    one single tree branching green...
        the steepled and misty moving distance.

    *

poplar trees slowly losing their lode of leaves ~
on the ground below, light pools swell with clarity.
   cattle lows ripple
    September ground fog,
     stirring the cinnamon-y tannic
     leaf rot musk of Autumn
      once again.

journal - 9/5/06

up before 6H - shook hands with Marc and as he had a mouthful of toothpaste foam, a muffled well-wishing. and i was off in the pale pink blue pre-dawn.

repeated the promenade to the Canal. surprised at the amount of people up and out at that early hour in such a small town... walking, biking, waiting for the bus. after all that shilly-shally back and forthing in the mind, the Canal was enchanting. and the autoroute that followed so close yesterday stayed well away today. the early morning smile-rich with grazing rabbits.

from across the bridgeless Canal i smelled the tell-tale aroma of sugary pastry baking, aaaaahhhhhh! torturous. crossed the Canal later at Montgiscard to a neighborhood commercial center. had a coffee in the cluttered chrome-bar-stooled bar watching the fat ripple round the frame of a heavy older lady sweeping. the classic assortment of syrups behind the counter and dusty photos of holiday drunk patrons hugging barkeeps on the wall.

continued down the kaleidocally tunneled sycamore-lined path overlaid with the hyper-Impressionistic light i always thought unreal in the paintings, but so real dappling here... flushing cyclists, trunks, those strolling and the very breeze with pastel tones. on and on and on and so shaded a chimp could swing for weeks from the Atlantic to the Mediterranean and never fear a leopard in the brush.

at the last lock before Toulouse... a café by the water. stopped for coffee and seeing my shell she gifted me an apple croustade with apple sorbet. i asked the distance - still 12K. "C'est rien," she laughs. "Deux enjambées." lock keeper across the Canal doing a Darwin Award-Charlie Chaplin saw-cut down the middle length of a picnic table he was standing on... i schadenfreudenly waited for the slapstick or goried conclusion, but neither occurred, so i carried on.

met a woman my age-ish coming the other way. she did le Chemin d'Arles - Camino Francés - Santiago, and back by the Camino Primativo du Nord... now on her return to Arles. easygoing with the laissez-faire casualness of the French. and she eased my mind about the Pyrénées mountain-crossing warnings in the guide. at some point there are cliffs below and above - but 'you just be careful.'

many multicolored and divers boat-house barges docked along the shaded Canal walls... jungle decor, neon and pastel painted, rusty, bamboo-ed, thatched, camouflage-tarped, rock music blaring with live teen-rage drum accompaniment. and again, as the sun got higher through the high-leavèd limbs... entrancing unfocus-edged dapplement of diffuse light beams on the water and the trail. again! an Impressionistic image i always thought just too delusive, that it was a lie of preference and style... but no. so real before me falling!

back in Toulouse!

never walked all the way around the Gare as the Canal goes. cut through the city when i saw a sign for centre-ville. passed through Place les Halles, Place Saint Georges, Place Wilson, to Rue Strasbourg... the statue of Jeanne d'Arc - right by le Clocher de Rodez where i stayed back in August, and to the hotel Raymond IV.

i know i'm losing that big toenail... the nail plate lifting up nicely now that i inattentively slammed it against a stone stoop ogling a palmier in a closed pastry shop window.

gentle meditation in the mismatched Cathedral with its monolithic central pillar. i half expect the whole stoney architecture to start rotating around this central axle like a toppled Ferris wheel.

lower towards the river i passed a bar with a green Basque Lauburu painted upon the entire outside wall and am here with a coffee and a beer before heading to la Truffe de Quercy restaurant, where i wanted to bring my family to feast during our overnight in Toulouse, before Sarlat - but we opted instead for simpler fare.

i don't know how i didn't get to the Quercy... but it was the long way. thought i had this city down. maybe it was the beer-softened sense of direction? fair soupe de poisson. excellent paté campagnard. and this cassoulet is slow roasted in a goblet-like bowl... duck confit, a sausage, pork belly strips and loads upon loads of creamy beans.

9/5/2006

    honey linden leaf-rot incense ~
the low morning sun lends
    autumnal hues to yet green leaves
        reflecting golden and flame pools
    upon le Canal de Midi...
last night's fried garlic
    expresses through teeth
    now working an almond croissant
        into perfect dissolution.

9/5/2006

stained-glass molten dawn light dapples
    the sage, mauve, and grey barked
        sycamore pillar rows whispering the Canal-long to Toulouse -
tracing trail with foot and mind patter...
burnt sugar pastry scent from the
    other bridgeless bank leaves me
        smiling at want.

journal - 9/6/06

spent a bit of distracted time at the cybercafé watching short videos of Steve Irwin's barb-in-the-heart stingray death, Jackass 2 previews, the sneezing baby panda scaring its mom, Geraldo smoking pot, the hysterical laughing Dutch baby...

...then headed to Église des Jacobins. wordy ole Thomas Aquinas' bones are bound and shelved in the altar foundation of this elatively high Gothic hall... the black marble floor expanse with a center row of fine pillars fanning up into carved stone ogive arches that burst into palm-like sprays against the brick ceiling. outside... a classic brick cloister of boxwood hedge maze-designs and clusters of spiring cypress... the galleried geometric tower rising between here and the blue skies. not so base a barrow, Thom!

soul and cell settling sit in the Basilique Saint Sernin. i still think the church is sterile but there's stable energy within. made a quick sketch of the outside of this afternoon's café and later, an attempt at the bridge. i keep learning - eye, coal, and thumb smudge.

i do love this pedestrian-friendly stretch of the city between the Canal and the Garonne. finally found a croix occitane i liked on that long pastry-scented street between Saint Sernin and Place de la Capitole. genial proprietor. commented on my accent. he mentioned that there's a Québecois poet who says one can see a country in an accent. missed much of what he had to say for the country in his, but got the gist. interesting comment about the attraction people have to the French Southwest. he said there have been racial beatings in the Southeast but not in the Southwest. for that he feels, mentally and energetically, that there's a more judicious air in these parts. glad to get an emblem of this region.

chose a restaurant called la Cave de Cassoulet... an underground brick-domed cavern. the waiter counseled me against ordering a middle course assuring that all their portions are 'énorme.' he slipped me a gift-dish of duck 'fritons,' - crispy salty duck fat chitlins! oooo so happy to have tooth and tongue! duck leg confit centered on the plate with three sides - potato gratin, haricots verts, and beets... each side split and placed around the plate like marking the hours of a gastronomic clock. and this is the best prune armagnac i've ever had. whole prunes soaked in armagnac, a breath of clove. the steeped brandy and three prunes swirling in a palm-warmed snifter.

heading back to the hotel... smells of leather and new clothes, fish market mussels on sweet mussel-juiced ice, sour spilt milk abandoned fridge, cigarets, piss and new printed bookstore paper, pastries, shwarma logs spit-rolling beside red element broiler coils - the incense of crisped roasting fat, salt and spice... falafel fried, coffee torrefacted, damp hookah peach tobaccos exhaled, curries, pit sweat and perfume. the ancient brick and mortar city baked and slowly eroding beneath today's 97º sun.

journal - 9/7/06

Musée des Augustins... down shaded cloister arcades extends a long row of upended gargoyles... grotesquely, like blind unfledged demonlings mewling for a talon tear of man-flesh. much of this museum's statuary has been collected from local church, basilica, and convent ecclesiaticals... the gargoyles, robed Brobdingnabian statues of bishops and saints, a hall of ornately sculpt and once significant pillar plinths and capitals... fissured frieze and entablature blocks prop open windows and emergency doors.

the city has a younger feel to it now. school and university are back in session. still hot late-night. poor Antonio must have told half of Toulouse how uncomfortable he is. heading off again tomorrow... a wave of lazy resistance. looks like only 23 stages until Puente la Reina. unlikely that i'll be in Saint-Jacques for my birthday, but who knows?

journal - 9/9/06

trudged with focused will up into the center. so grateful for this Pibrac stop a mere 15K away. still feeling poison's pain. after i got the rickety, (but veneered-anew), room above the bar, i made my ablutions and chugged some water. lying down after washing clothes the sweat started pouring out of my body... POURING! making me think there were still plenty of toxins there-in releasing. i soaked the sheets and had to hang them on a chair to dry... felt like a July ice sculpture!

two days ago, my 'last' night in Toulouse, i got a sandwich from the Casino Grocery to tide me over until a salad and pizza fantasy later... Jimmy loves his pizza. roamed about, sat on the fountained plaza and drew the Cathedral facade, noting i wasn't getting hungry. idled by the river then began to recognize the all too familiar food poisoning feel... the slow stomach roll and sharp wince in the jaw hinge. by sheer mind control i made the long trek back to the Raymond IV and, just seconds through the door, was puking with brutal force and bounty... whole body-wracking pain set in... the knotted spine-lining muscles the force of retching tore through... fever... shakes. even at 4H i could hardly make it to the bathroom without the aid of concentrated breath and hands to stabilizing walls. kept sipping water and watching repetitively distractive CNN... all 'Steve Irwin and the Ray' coverage. those talking heads sure can wring the marrow out of a story. Pakistan cedes a border region to the Taliban, Taliban is rolling in a bumper crop of poppies, Israeli blockade is finally over. how much money is rebuilding Lebanon going to cost? Darfur... how many homes destroyed and resettlement forced? and why? the panting Hounds of Hatred know no rest the world round... shadows and snuffling at the crack of light beneath the door.

shuffled downstairs to the reception desk at 8H to ask for another night... trembling with fever and worry. i didn't think i could make it to another hotel, or even another room, without assistance. in bed all day. went out at 18H with feet so gently falling on the sidewalk so's to stir nothing within. fissuring headaches.

up at 8H and still far from prime. glad i bought that expensive map three days ago as it had plans of the city outskirts as well. suburbia... passed right by the airport into Colomiers and then found it difficult to get out, like the directions were written 'contrariwise' in Wonderland - lefts for rights, turns for straight-aheads. man filling up at the gas station helped me find the D24... the hot highway straight into Pibrac...

...and straight into the arms of Sainte Germaine... the gentle peasant shepherdess with an apron full of roses, whose statue in chapel, church and Cathedral has always made me wonder on who she was. in the numinous energetic family that we all belong to, that thrives from within us through to the universe without, i believe the representational figures of our saints and spiritual teachers concentrate the energy they evoked and lived, and that through insight this focused energy can be tapped for our own healing and learning. every apple has learned from every blossom for every season ever since Bloom bloomed, and i am glad to have come across her mythology here, where she tended land and lamb... a simple peasant saint of the people... a woman disfigured and shunned yet ever compassionate... a fragment of Mary and Kuan Yin reflected.

"Where there is great love there are always miracles. Miracles rest not so much on the faces or voices or healing power coming from afar off, but upon our being made finer so that for a moment our eyes can see and our ears can hear what is there about us always," Willa Cather says, and i agree.

there's a local association fair going on on the tree-lined promenade between the hilltop church and Basilica... no products - mainly clubs: gymnastics, tai chi, alpine cycling, mountain climbing, moto... about 20 tents. the beer tent is the only one i visited. had a few opaque plastic cupfuls while at the journal, then drew the Église Sainte Marie-Madeleine facade until dusk.

this deliciously crappy pizza from across the street is the first thing i've eaten since the salmonella sandwich eructations. called the OT to reserve. guess there's someone else who called... the Chemin is changing faces.

journal - 9/10/06

i really liked that rickety refurbished hotel last night. i have an affinity for the rickety. the warm honey pineboard walls... so quiet after Toulouse. even with the double windows closed tight there, there was still that muffled metropolis' somewhere-activity-of-sound. wonderful, here, to have the windows wide open and silence blowing in.

the dark morning going slowly blue and rose as was want for Sainte Germaine's domain. the trail passed by the church, orangely illuminated among the cedars, and backed down off the pious hill, crossed train tracks, wended through trees giving bough-arched and arbored peeks into misty meadows... then by Sainte Germaine's grotto - flowers fresh and gone to parchment, melted wax stalactites, -mites and dribbled harlequin shards mark an age of intentions prayed. someone's last-of-the-wick votive whispering eloquent shadows against chapel walls before the silencing day's sun rises.

the negatives... the Sunday fields were full of aggressive hunting dogs and gunshot reports... the woods full of sudden 'leap out of the way or i'll mow you down' cyclists in bright skintights, and those infernal Metta black flies in front of brow and eyes no matter what i did! ease of mind, ease of mind, ease of mind. and all day seeing naught but the inside of a forest... naught but the underside of leaves.

the positives... as the day ended, the trail followed a high and narrow hillcrest road that gave, on either side, to fields, farms and tree-tucked homes below. the scent of shorn crops and tillage drying in the humid wind blowing in from away. ah, breath.

as she said on the phone, the l'Isle-Jourdain gîte was on the way out of town... wicked on the way out, actually. curious as to why the OT and the gîte aren't closer to the center but there's the 'base de loisirs' out here on the outskirts... a soccer field or two, a campground, a municipal pool, a few man-made lakes. there's also an entangled round-a-bout intersection of directions nearby so i guess it makes sense. how pleased they'll be with my approval.

opened up the gîte. that someone else called to reserve had me sure it was crazy Antonio... but what to my wondering eyes! OG! the old guy from Gallargues and Tendonitis Ivan from la-Salvetat!

the gîte is in a semi-refurbished and falling apart building amidst composite pool-area structures and is not far from looking graffiti sprayed and beer-can strewn in the urban bus stop sense. a shabby cobwebbed kitchen. saw an old-fashioned 'the cartoon's true!' mouse trap with a hard cheese stone on the tender trigger.

healed heels showing red wear spots. this corporeal erosion never ends! frequent sick to my stomach acid-strong quease contractions today... remnants of sour microbes' brutal assault.

Ivan also slept on the Baziège Presbytery floor... saw roaches. said the mattress room smelled like cat piss. didn't like Generous Movie Man and he didn't have a pleasant exchange with Sparks at the waterworks gîte, either... but he did have a sweet time in Joncels. what an oasis!

9/10/2006

warm and field-mist-smoothed
    rose morning light -
        such sweet night's
        sleep in the soles of my feet
            for walking,
    for walking westward,
        the blue white moon.

9/10/2006

morning meadow
        liquid moonlight mist -
a sweat bead trickles
        elbow
            stopping walking
to peer the forest fringe for deer.

9/10/2006

left early, hiked for hours,
    to the marrow beat.
        even thoughts are yawnful -
wanting to nap - hearing wind snake sounds
    through sere sun-dried
        September hays,
and i am consumed...
    the me-paunched ouroboros
        dozes in a pine.

journal - 9/11/06

up early. left first. went the wrong way twice in darkness. kept staring at the map until it made sense and i hopped a fence, the tracks, a hedge and made quick time to Monferran-Savès. quiet main street lined with potted-plant packed sidewalks no one ever trods on and amber stucco walls. the number of mentally handicapped centers seems disproportionate to the size of the town. one torque-toothed smiling man ran gangly limbs over to me and started talking purely, without hindrance of heart. he must have been the ring-leader as others from the Center soon came out to inspect and question me, shake my hand and ask me about the trail. a little village. a little touch.

another day of easy-on-the-eye agricultural rolling hills, crops gone, forgotten ears of corn drying strangely on the stalks. drying sunflower fields, the leaves all black like the frost hit hard... down-gazing heads swelling with weighty obsidian seeds.

vallonée, vallonée, vallonée... smooth ups and smooth downs... white tracked trails and grassy... winding by farm houses and their bitch-ass dogs. a pheasant runs away from me. always away. bang a left or right anytime ya dummy, you keep running in front away and frantically squawking like the old-time country biddies who unbutton bosom down a notch and unlock doors hearing a ravager's escaped and near.

tramped into Gimont wishing in my heart success for Clarisse's gîte endeavor. a coffee on the tippy wooden deck that could use a planer and a shim. sausages grilling inside... fat spattering bright flame-ups behind the bar and rumbling storm thunderhead responses.

arrived in la Motte and there's comfortable feeling here and warm colors. their dogs barked then left me alone. the struggle over a ham bone - psychological greed spans the species! an older grey dog gnawing, nestled in the thick green grass... the younger, from well within the house, came peering out the fly beads at the sound and bounded over to take it away - then left it, it not being fought for. wisdom smiling in the old dog's eyes as he lies back down on the lawn to recommence his osseous feast.

these folks are cool, though i've only met Martine. they refurbish and build houses naturally... there's dirt between the upstairs floor and downstairs ceiling for insulation, they make their own bricks, and their walls are haybales strengthened with wooden frames - waterproofed, stuccoed over and painted in warm North African colors. through the entryway a golden adobe four-arched dome inhales me in to a sofa-lined sitting room just begging for a book and a rainy day. a star mosaic constellates the floor with a bare footprint image. this gîte acts as their display showroom. so tempted to stay another day. it's living material, living insulate walls, it is of the earth and essential.

Didier, the Old Guy, showed up while i was washing my clothes out back... scrubbing Vaseline out of a greasy underwear crotch, picking a sun-warm fig... scrubbing skanky socks, picking a sun-warm fig... scrubbing out pit sweat and shoulder strap stink, picking a sun-warm fig. "on n'est pas riche," but how we celebrate makes the day.

Ivan arrived later while i was cooking my stew. fried garlic, onions and carrots until golden... added tomato, zuchini, the garbanzos with their liquid, a can of tuna, some rosemary and whole coriander... scrumptious. Ivan took the long way around Gimont... ups and downs and under bridges i never saw. and for his detour he was starving! ate a 2-lb steak he lugged up from a supermarché - which i also didn't see.

journal - 9/12/06

i was hook and sinker staying in la Motte another rest day... right until the moment i sat up and said "let's go." can't linger in every euphoric corner i come across. let it become a memory and a longing. reheated my stew leftovers with Martine's two vocal cats cheek-and-jowling my ankles. buckled up. thanked her again. i admire what she's done and doing here. and went off down the path again, whistling David Banner's haunting refrain.

much the same day visually. steep hill climbs, then following easy ridge crests down. sometimes scrub brush sheltered... sometimes oak growth and berry bush lined. tractors shuttlecock their tilling earthen wakes from hilltop to valley, hilltop to valley, churning the earth... day after day after day harrowing huge earth boulders down to stone-size, fist-size, fingers and finally to pea-size grains so to be receptive for next year's planting. all a variously textured spackle across the hillsides.

passed several beam-and-stucco manses built for the generations... that first one in Lanne surrounded by feathery elegant pine boughs splayed out in golden morning light... boughs sheltering a mother and daughter gathering flower stems in the garden below. their bear-shouldered blond dog arose at my approach but she lumbered my way only to sniff and be pet. later a dog did actually charge and hit my shoulder braced staff, then backed off gnashing black-gummed incisors. another squat-towered manor overlooking till-patterned hillsides... its masoned stone and blood-red shutters claiming false permanence against the immense white cloud mass billowing behind.

from there-on the Chemin didn't read the guide. it roughly followed the same direction, but nothing corresponded until the Couloumé Park... and i took in the impressioning view of Auch from down below with its bluff-cresting Cathedral and fortified walls overlooking the river.

got in at 13H. a note tacked to the Presbytery's locked door suggested that the OT gave access to the gîte at 14H, but they seemed to know nothing of this. 'Would you like a map?' me peevishly thinking, no i want a friggin' shower. got the tampon at the Cathedral but never made it back to sit or visit. bought an imaginary almond croissant because the bloody shop was closed and i spat gall on this lazy country for a while chewing on a grilled vegetable panini... bereft amidst plenty, poor lamb.

the gîte occupies the top floor of this monolithic stone Presbytery capping a cliff beside the Cathedral. gorgeous! best views of the mottled clay-tile roofs avalanching down to the green banked Gers. the royalty of high ceilings and windows masoned within towering stone, eye-level with hawks sculling wings. Didier and i are here. he has a disturbingly turgid blister on the ball of the foot giving him grief so i offered to do his shopping.

on the way back from the grocery... menacing dark and not so distant clouds. arriving upstairs, Didier was battening down the floor-to-ceiling window-shutter hatches and had hauled our laundry in from the balcony before it blew away and became prayer flag rags on the ariel antennas down below. receiving the groceries he smiled a slow and heavily accented English "Tank yoo, Jeem."

and as i eventually settled into my café table and chair, the sky tore open with lightning roars and wind-driven rain erasing the sound of the fountain. nearly an hour's storm and it has since cooled down.

European mourning doves... whistle this - whoo whoooo who... whoo whoooo who... where the second 'who' trails with a curlicue diphthong and the third is curt.

the Universe began by sautéing onions, garlic and carrots. sautéed onions, garlic and carrots... added peanuts, diced apples... soon the tomatoes and lentils went in... and someone's leftover greens. waiting for each added layer to cook on the low-watted hotplate i sewed my daypack zipper, torn a few days ago... sittin', simmerin', stitchin' ...listenin' to the rain.

9/12/2006

stalk crops lie in tilled
    dragon-bone shard rows,
        among crumble earth clods
        thinning tree shade reaches toward
      another horizon-wide afternoon September sky.

journal - 9/13/06

woke when i heard Didier leaving. he's slow at 72 and is always up at 5H and out by 7H. for his easy movements i think he got up late-night and burst his blister. should have done that a while ago. glad my bed was by the door. with this brooding overcast i might have slept until 9H.

from the heights of the Presbytery windows the near distance fades in fog, narrow wet amber-lit streets below and embery floodlights still illuminate the Cathedral... the glowing and grey buttress stones in coal-bright relief against a clouded sky...

reheated the stew remains for breakfast and left as the kids were headed to school. followed a campestral lane winding through last night's rain-swashed valleys and hills, through foggy forests, and into a spicy leaf-rot poplar grove. morning firearms in woods and fields. dwelling on interdependence and interbeing i ate the wild yellow apple that thud before me on the trail, mealy-sweet and gone in three bites small... white hourglass core tossed into September-brown fern berms.

a light rain fell several times freshening brow. passed an 'élevage de gibier,' a game farm with ferocious Shepherds guarding deer and curled horn sheep. with military precision two hounds took to the fence and one held the high-ground against my 'aggression!'

today's subtle change... while there is still plenty of agriculture - there's less. more land is left to wild-growth spaces.

as i crossed the bridge into Barran i spied Didier in the distance, heading to the bar... erroneously to where the guide said Madame Coco kept the gîte key. Madame Coco reigns as a self-important Guppy in a piddling village pond and she insisted on keeping our crédencials for a while for her persnickety perusal. the only person in all of France and Spain to do so. and with all that can happen between 'now' and 'then' ...Didier, who did the Chemin a few years ago, (people are recognizing him along the way), Didier arrived in Barran on the exact same date he did last time! Coco, of course, had it documented.

she took us over to the gîte. sagging barn doors groan swinging open to the mote-bemothed barn space and barn garage behind... up the dry two flights of stairs dropping dust-puffs with each footfall... down a hallway of rustic, formerly schoolroom rooms... rows of wall-taped elementary school-kids' drawings with their medieval misproportions and smiling suns... shards of the garage space below visible through gapped floorboards. four cots - a hot plate - a powerful shower.

friendly golden mutt by the arched entry to Barran and a coy calico cat here on the restaurant's windowsill. the tension to flee or be pet trembling her nape and hesitant paw. the cozy restaurant... still a few boots-a-table patrons there when i strolled in earlier. my movement a magnet in the many-eyed room. a snippet in the tabac-presse next door says in the XIXth Century Barran was famous for 'snail production.' with them they used to make therapeutic gums to prevent people from coughing. what an odd (read: repulsive) alchemical thought to have.

this is another place that has that isolated feel but which probably isn't. with the church's helically twisted bell-tower, called a flèche flammée - only about a hundred of that style left in Europe, and the quaint well-kept town with its XVth Century arched entryway by the River Baïse - it has to be a touristic destination.

while Didier was washing up i bedded down with a night-making t-shirt over my eyes and in an instant i was out. OUT! could have stripped and dyed me blue, i'd have never known.

waking... Didier is nowhere to be seen.

leaning back against a lamppost i tried to draw the flèche flammée...

journal - 9/14/06

felt bad switching on the one overhead light this morning. Didier didn't mind. he told me to "Allumez si vous voulez," after hearing me stumble in the dark. but Ivan ate out at the restaurant and came in late. Dids was sleeping in per the doctor, (that's where he was), who made some sort of incision in the foot and used a syringe to extract impacted pus. the Doc iodined him, fit him with a dressing and a mesh sock to keep it secure so the lesion could breathe and dry, and prescribed a rest day. wanting to make sure i got to Montesquiou before the grocery closed midday to stock up for Pouylebon, i clicked the light on. sorry Ivan. and set out just before 7H... just as the first few drops of rain began to fall...

and they haven't stopped.

passed a pungent élevage de canards. would have made a bonny shot with all the white ducks...100's of them squawking against the green hillside. but i'm not taking my Lomo out of its swaddle of plastic bags in this deluge. trails sunken between the fields and canopied with vegetation - les chemins creusés they're called - blue berried paxarán shrubs and red rosehipped branches bent overhead for the weight of rain...

arrived just after 10H in Montesquiou to take advantage of the well-stocked and warrening grocery, then went to the bar for a café crème and called the gîte. first time i left a message, second time she picked up... "Pas de souci." 'No worries. Come on down.'

bartender is a friendly codger with an intense Southwest accent. we looked at the Météo in La Dépêche du Midi... tomorrow - rain and clouds. Saturday - clouds. Sunday - sun.

about a K off the trail... a home among trees and fields. the gîte is a corrugated roofed 'hangar' so many farms have... a two-storey wall-less roof typically erected to protect equipment and wood and hay from the elements. these folks have walled in the sheltering roof and built seemingly crate-stacked rooms in two corners - outside the rooms the space is arranged like when suburbanites turn their garage into a summer living room... plastic patio furniture and nylon-webbed lounge chairs, brown painted picnic tables with spiderweb nested underbellies... a few cots scattered out here too, for warmer days. once integral, now 'decor obsolete' farm hand-equipment adorns the walls. their money-cat-colored greyhound peering at me through the window.

no let up with the rain. a constant and far-field reaching sound... wrapped in a comforter writing.

made another bang-up stew... onion, carrot, garlic, leftover salami, apple, tomato, zuchini and a can of lentils. a few minutes after 20H... still raining. whittled at toe and plantar slough for a while. dried my clothes by the space heater and drove their bill up a bit... sorry Charlie. pardon Charles.

9/14/2006

field, leaves, and hat brim
    give batter to September rain

    *

summer purple thistle torches
    gone weathered silver-grey

    *

yet standing amber cornstalk row flames
    flank hillsides
        as in bygone siege days

       *

red rosehips glow holes in woolly spiderwebs
    and my boots are slicked golden with this land's mud

       *

the sea i'm walking far to
    falling here.
wondering if i'll make it past tonight's
    roof, bed, stew, tea, and sleep…
        is there a special fork in dream we take to waken anew.

9/14/2006

Got mule dust on my fingers,
    blisters on my heels.
Railway Crossing red-lights flashing
    rhythmic crash of metal wheels.

       *

Blackbird-burled-tree limbs so silent,
    smell the coming mountain rain.
Wonder where i'll sleep tonight,
    fruit fall rotting in the shade.

9/14/2006

last night's hard rain
    absorbed, expressed...
the vegetative sweet-spice scented earthen breath and
    milky mist veils soften
        eyes against today's rolling quilt-rumpled
            Gers hillsides.
the wild, the shorn, the tilled...
    broad color and form sweeps in seeping
        watercolor detail.
    my mind drifts to the last time it rained ~
sound of antique organ pipes' stops and keys, like tocking a
    mallet
on a bone xylophone,
    the Lodève Cathedral breathing.
  a day's drive
but spirit-foot ages away ~
  j'arrose la rosée,
    i water the dew,
      pissing in wet morning grass
        may not be new...
    but i like it.

journal - 9/15/06

cracked my window open to the garage-room space to listen to the rain pound down on the corrugated and to give that shadow-casting daddylonglegs a way out. the storm battered and battered and harder still against the windows. how cozy it feels to lie here and be dry. a lulliful sleeping sound. a profound sleep.

breakfasted on leftover stew and fruit and headed out. she could have told me about the shortcut back. after the rain - the mud. gold mud. instant cement that clots in the boot treads and makes walking like walking on rounded soles... unbalancing through the vertebra-piled spine. it doesn't take a genius to turn that mire into building bricks.

long stretch in the woods to Pouylebon's XIth Century simple church facade glowing amber in the low morning light. the narrow single-apsed hilltop Église Saint Christaud overlooking lower rolling hills... advancing towards, the rising sun behind, and the curve of the earth ahead stretched my shadow scythed-Reaper black cloakly and long.

in the courtyard of the Monlezun Mairie i startled a quail grazing on golden pebbles and it bolted wings away over the wall, gliding high above fields shorn and tilled. and i longed jealously for flight... to soar like that at surprised will. traversed similar countrysides the soaring quail saw the daylong...

...daylong and into Marciac. towering black thunderheads gathering above the café on the playingfield-wide square. more Brit voices - another enclave! looking forward to the day here.

the caretakers are friendly folks with an overgrown backyard garden... wisteria walls, hollyhocks, prolific limb-bent fruit trees, compost piles rising with September labor. a barn-loft type gîte... dorm-cot spaces divided by curtains which the open-window winds animate... windows giving on to the glowingly gold-stoned church steeple surrounded by cedar limbs... hydrangea shrubs in scattered acidic blue bloom below. don't really know if i had a nap or a meditation there in the church, but it was restful. more ribbon-bound inspirational messages in a basket by the mossy holy water font.

just off the main square is a directional road sign for the D3 heading to Aire-sur-l'Adour! years ago in Aire i had a moving experience upon entering the dimly lit XIth Century church with bells gonging 3:00 in the afternoon... that soaring YoYo Ma-Bach 'Suite for Solo Cello in G Major' piece sounding through scratchety speakers... and reading a quote from Jesus i had not heard before

- "Venez a l'écart et reposez-vous un peu." 'Come away from the crowd and rest for a while.' a triptych that strummed emotion in my heart. and here and now, standing beside the mossy stone holy water font in silence my scrolled note said - "Mais Jésus leurs dit, 'C'est moi, n'ayez pas peur.'" which in Christian terms is the non-Christian meditation i've been using for much of the way... circling to the sacred center of all things and looking them in the eye... the pupils' symbiotic reflections. if i am reminded it is because i have forgotten. funny, the mind... find a new way to practice presence and distraction shifts into over-drive.

drew the Marciac plaza... then the steeple. i don't know how to use color and am going to toss those pencils. kid came over while i was sketching the tower with charcoal, thumb and eye. told him it wasn't working out... showed him the previous steeple - "O c'est joli!" i love kids.

saw Ivan's bag.

a table at Le Coin Gourmand, sipping wine with Ossian and reflecting on these days... this September wind, the winds of autumnal change from the Mediterranean's high vaporous cloud-front waves come crashing down to thicken the air here below... the swelling humidity feeding the essence of the season.

the crops are gone... summer's swollen cornstalks now are crumbling rootball clods... wheats, reap seeds and oats are shorn down to stubble against hard-packed earthen rows trickling with green weed streams. the tractor passing, passing, re-passing... harrowing down the clumped remains, amber cab-light flickering rhythmic pulses importantly while the farmer's wife, without ego's beacon, does the same to flour, butter and a pinch of salt with two knives in a bowl... harrowing the dough down into pea-size clumps for crusts to receive the fruits of the season... to transform the fruits of the season into jams, pies, croustades and crisps... the pickled, puréed and stewed. field and kitchen parallels and the belly sings!

this is the energy of the place and season... with cram-full chipmunk cheeks grinning, what's been brought forth has been borne away to fill granary, hayloft and pantry. and the Earth's seasonal breath, now on the deep inhale, gathers cinnamon tannic leaf rot, wild fruit fall fermentation musk, vegetal compost scents, unculled sunflower and cornfield spice, hunters' feathers and offal left behind... gathering, gathering, inhaling for the long Winter's sleep! inhaling and hiking through this shade lessening season... hiking the hilly quilt-rumpled landscape, climbing steep and high then winding crests deep valley downward to do it all over again... climbing steep and high and winding easy hillcrest ways down across the rolling Gers countryside... the rains cooling forest and field, vapors rising. and that was a meal!

chèvre chaud, foie gras maison, confit de canard with wine-roasted mushrooms and a fine bottle of Madiran. a tisane in the cigaret clouded salon.

journal - 9/16/06

in the fieldstone and barn-board anteroom between the owner's house and the upper gîte rooms... stacks of refuse lumber and piled tools, counter, sink, chipped dishes and hot-pot, the granite threshold step to backyard gardens. Madame spread the table with a country-style petit déj of thick crusted breads, homemade sugar-boiled plum and strawberry jams, coffee, cheese - and outside, the rain. glad i didn't shove off this morning.

went to buy a newspaper and read watching the flagstoned square spatter silver wet sparks.

bought fixin's for a guacamole sub... my reverend tomato, onion, avocado and cheese creation whose calorics have fired my flesh across many a countryside. and as the unofficial temperature is moving well past chilly into cold i bought a fleece at the GamVert. Ivan bought waterproof pants and promptly broke the cheap snaps.

can he talk! ...and he knows it. calls himself a "moulin à mot." he phoned ahead earlier and apparently the private gîte is full, so he reserved two places in a caravan at the Camping for us. i appreciate it, but tomorrow might be a manageable day to do a double étape.

read / nap / rain / nap / café / read / nap / café / rain... this is a rest day so rest.

when i arrived yesterday i talked over restaurant possibilities with a couple of Brit cyclists outside the Café Hôtel de Ville. parting, he said a frictionless something. "May your God go with you." love that ecumenical tone. inside Café Hôtel de Ville now... the rain's doing a serious rataplan, paradiddle and blur across the arcaded plaza... glassy-eyed bartender pours me a Jameson's... tallest in France. must be getting closer to Spain. the pours in France hardly wet the lips and cost you 9E to hardly do so.

the acronym here is JIM! 'Jazz in Marciac.' and looking at the August schedule my aural friend from la Traviata in Cáceres, Bebo Valdés, performed here. and Winton Marsalis is a frequent.

i think in 6-7 days i'll be in Spain.

ate my canned sardines, VacBox veggie soup and tomato, mozzarella and olive salad... the owner's cat inviting herself onto my warm lap. together we felt our bodies expand and soften with breath... together we listened to the rain, aware we are warm and dry.

journal - 9/17/06

the body felt energized - a strong day of thigh and stride after that day of rainy rest. was concerned about cementish mud combined with the distance of the double étape so i took the shorter way. the D943 out of Marciac is a narrow country road winding under a crisp September sky... not crisp enough to use my new fleece, but there is a bite in the air.

crossing loud rain-gorged streams and rivers... corn crops, forests and fields. all similar landscapes until, from around a high blind bend i got my first glimpse of the Pyrénées Range angling westward... colossal snow white peaks and lower taluses blue with distance - a whole-body flush of excitement. lost the view later for the clouds and lower altitudes but the image of the moon-raking range was in me.

taking this shorter way i got to Maubourguet early... 10H, and there's a grocery open on a Sunday! now there's a miracle to convert me quicker than loaves and fishes. Maubourguet is thriving with mountain energy... a base for sporting day-excursions into the mountains and the local commerces reflect those interests L.L.Bean-cataloguely. called the gîte from the sycamore-lined square... nonchalant, 'Yeah, the door's open.' followed the riverbank to the church... old man hanging over his stonewall watching what the swollen river passes by.

it got hilly soon afterwards. September Sunday gun shots, men shouting, dogs bay... peeking through the trees i watched a hunter rifle down something wounded on the ground.

much cursing in mind as no one in these parts closes their gates or chains their friggin' dogs. should i pass through here again i'm bringing arsenic and a steak. at least four times today the bloodthirsty curs 'escorted' me off their territory.

dirt track high in the wooded hills outside Vidouze. two Grey-Bearded Brit Brothers stopped their rust bucket jeep and in accentless French asked me if i was on the Chemin? "Yes I am!" i Englishly intoned like the Bud Light commercial they've never seen. younger Brother has a home and gîte in Arriagosse - said he had a pilgrim to Lourdes show up in the pitch black rain three days before Christmas once. been off the grid there for about six years. warm-hearted talk. meaningless words. profound contact.

the gîte in Anoye is located behind the Mairie, and together they share the surrounding cobblestone plaza ringed with limb-entangled plane trees. notably clean dorm and kitchen the residents must use for local functions and feasts, i'm guessing, for the amount of silverware and the size of the thick bottomed pots. hospitalier passed by later for the fee, the tampon, and to show me the fridge which offers a door-load of provisions for sale... beer, soda, fruit juice, cheeses, butter. there are other more substantial food-stuffs locked up which the hungry pilgrim can buy when the 'responsable' passes. plenty of wine too.

journal - 9/18/06

the kitchen's exterior door was mounted with an Exit light that gave a eerie green glow to that room beyond. thought sure i'd wake to a knife-wielding silhouette of Michael or Jason in the dorm doorway.

my alarm beeped at 7H and i'm out. the gold-fissured clouds and blue sky bays soon succumbed to dark cloud banks, and further away hillsides went gauzy with mist fall. rain never truly gathered strength and these were simply passing veils.

followed a narrow tar lane threading agricultures, hamlets, communes and farmhouse clusters. more dogs - incredible! as soon as i crossed into the Haute-Pyrénées department people stopped using leashes. more thoughts of TASERs and Mace.

so many cornfields gone to pot. i do not understand growing corn to let it rot. it pisses me off. aren't people starving to death? and out of work? can no one but slugs and crows use the fruit of such labor? grist that grain! build a still! France is the size of Texas. are you telling me they, (or UNICEF, or the WHO, or ECHO, or the beneficent arm of the EU), can't assemble a migrant team of Combines to rove the countrysides this time of year and gather what the farmers give up on? pure lack of imagination.

down one trail, shaking her head with the disparaging attitude of 'what are you people doing?' ...an AWOL cow sitting squat in the middle of the track watching her fellow fenced-in bessies down below, all shoulder-deep in floodwater muck, surround a metal haybale holder and chaw and chaw and jostle, slosh and chaw. upon her suddenly from behind she looked like a Charles Williams sinewy-backed lioness and the sayonara thought crossed me mind that o this is the end... the Forms have stepped down from beyond to crush us.

stopping to admire a section of wild and wooded that was, aberrantly for the season, still in bloom, i was ambushed by a horrible conceit of creation... a part-fly, part-mosquito, part-tick, part-succubus with bulbous eyes. couldn't brush it off, the legs clung so. horrible beast. i need a pet bat on a leather lash.

more trail sections today were unmowed and untended... farmers' Fall focus is on tilling the fields, not grooming the trails between them. paused to talk with one agèd farmer on the road. HE, at least, has a mellow yellow hound. on the approach i watched it sniff the knobbed tractor tires with glaze-eyed attention. bet he can distinguish each cow whose manure stuck in the treads. farmer talked about a few pilgrims he's met as the Chemin used to go by his house, but it moved. his strong Midi accent is tellingly trillée... the r's rippled like in Spain and Québec.

made it to Morlaàs in the mist. you can't outmaneuver the unknown. wanted to be 'in town' and the cheap hotel i found is further away than the Camping. bought a Rando Chemin Français guide for Spain! and since the corner store is closed the woman at the tabac-presse-librarie showed me the way to a Super-U. a chocolate bar with crème brulée crunchy filling is the highlight of purchases. and i bought heavy-duty tape to line the inner boot against the Achilles heel. hoping maybe that will cut down on some friction and help the flesh that has eroded heal. worth a try.

the light was glowingly perfect on the church's elaborate stone tympanum... took several precise depth-of-field Lomo shots of it with the roiling dark clouds behind. happy to have gleaned that from the day.

called home to wish Mom and Dad a happy anniversary and told them the story... a woman in the tourist office asked where i was from. i told her Maine is just south of Québec. "Oh," she says, "Castine?" how the hell do you know Castine? behind my eyes is what i'm thinking. there's nothing there but the Maine Maritime Academy, a bar, and ocean shredding rocky coasts. apparently through the old inheritance custom of Entail and Primogeniture - i.e. the oldest son gets it all while the rest get screwed... one of the younger 'screwed' rakish sons of the local Castin family made his way to the New World - got himself a native bride, had a slew of kids and founded Castine. that's just weird.

9/18/2006

rested and rain-day sated,
    thighs swing arms
        and torso-strapped backpack strongly
    across countryside
        and through villages in Sunday silence slowly
            simmering to a bustle...
    café - coffee.
  pâtisserie - chocolate tresse.
rivers, fields, and cloud puff blue skies
        all sea-froth me forward
           to the white capped
                Pyrénées' loom

    *

sun-gold fissured cloud floes,
        a rooster crows
            to ruffle off
      mid-September's dew and chill ~
wild chestnut groves
      swell and swing light green spiny fruit
          above the trail,
   forgotten on the stalk corn rows
           for a while
   and then these lines of mine...
this body not my true body rots,
    measured out in walking staff length
        strokes and
  this meditation on all
        i see is
the true body this body-not-my-body
        will become,
   zygote to th' universal womb...
      the true body i will become.

       *

      holly berries' sharp green waxen leaves,
         forestral sparks
            between hillock and sun.

       *

hard boot soles crackle acorns walking in oaken shade.
       *

    hidden mossy bridge,
        hidden wet branch trail,
            unrepeatable brook liquiding
                laughter,
      mist sheets through
          corn leaves' soft sounds...
these forest, field, and dog-fang haunted hamlet days.

journal - 9/19/06

sky barely more blue than black when i left kicking through wind-rustling sycamore leaf piles.

leaving Morlaàs through neighborhood shortcut woods and fields of corn... "Fait beau aujourd'hui!" a hunter said smiling from the dewy field in knee-boots... the Pyrénées, more jagged than before, on the nearing horizon. some peak - maybe Pic d'Aspe, where i'm headed, is like a single saw-toothed incisor among the spaces. where field and forest meet in bramble an old-timer with oxygen tank and nose tubes on a bike talks to an old-timer in a truck. as i approached them his dog approached me. "N'est pas méchant," Nose Tubes said... Truck said, "Il mange pas la viande de cul," ...he doesn't eat ass meat!

through replanted recreational forests with numbered allées...

...and into the well-kempt streets of Lescar's medieval center. the XIIth Century Cathédrale de Notre Dame, her high-walled cemetery, and ramparts and ruins of a once episcopal palace's tower line a small ridge overlooking green playing fields below.

pumped up the pulse getting here before the OT closed at noon... got the key, and the gîte is perfect! two bunkbed dorm rooms, a well-stocked and clean kitchen, a locked gate, a locked door, and! for the first time in 3 1/2 months it looks like i'll use a washer / dryer.

i laid out breakfast and arranged the veg for 'potage pèlerin' tonight... gonna buy some thyme but the secret ingredients are hunger and fresh air.

a still meditation with the organ in the Cathedral. behind the altar, roped off on the floor, there's a XIIth Century mosaic of an archer with a peg-leg in mid-draw... interesting, but shadowy to observe. back at the gîte i met Frike, a Belgian woman, and Didier was there! and we shared my dinner of pilgrim stew with thyme.

journal - 9/20/06

nearly wriggling with a three-year-old's glee... i forgot i had - and didn't share - and so still have to rapture! my crunchy crème brulée chocolate bar. bonne job Lindt!

Frike and Didier left silently, left me a well-wishing note, an orange, the disgusting paté and a few yogurts. i pocketed the orange and reheated my stew with some leftover wine. packed up and headed out over the train tracks, hunter yelling at his hounds to stay away from me...

up blood-pumping steep switchbacks in the woods by more palombiers - those high tree shack-blinds used to hunt doves from October 1st to November 15th... not without protest and contention - eco-warriors firebomb the tree stands!

warm morning and my feet hit the tarmac here in Lacommande just as the 11:30H bell sounded.

mind often still with bird sounds, rauque and sweet, repetitive and singular. mind often tripping on am i wasting a day here not pushing on to Oloron? woman near the Mairie is the 'responsable' for the gîte. a note above her doorbell not to ring - "bébé qui dort." the pilgrim who slept here last night left late and she's apologetic for not having cleaned up yet. a small camp-like four-bedded gîte. a hot-plate and salt. glad i packed some of Lescar's butter in an empty Yop bottle. someone left a bag of wild walnuts i cracked open and toasted in a pan.

after washing self and clothes i set both out to dry in the detergent-ad-worthy sunny breeze.

roamed about - a residential commune with decorative banana palms and rose bushes, roadside embankments full of blade-leaved yucca stalks in white bell-blossomed profusion... and homes' fading flower gardens seeming to say, 'i've done my seed proliferation duty for the season. thank you.' and with a kiss quickly to loved ones be done.

mourning doves, roosters and dog bays mark the distance. and i'll try to draw this black-slate-towered church and bastion from the XIIth Century... a relais on the trail and part of a former network of hospitals giving aid to the pilgrims - not all made it. 800-year-old gravestone steles sporadically mushroom through the grass. cooking and eating look to be the highlights of Lacommande, but peace and quiet reign. warm green hillsides and deep respiration... gather the silence Spain tends not to have.

going inside to get more tea... the gîte smelled of roasted nuts. will have to prepare the rest of them to leave for later people.

butter fried the onions and carrots to the slow resistor pulse of a radiant-and-fade, radiant-and-fade hot-plate coil... added the garlic and salt. having nothing else for liquid i used two cups of strong cinnamon-orange black tea, stirred rice into risotto, added the mushrooms, the toasted walnuts and thyme...

9/20/2006

sun-toasted corn on the cob in
    the husk on the
        stalk
        scent ~
            mourning dove,
              morning mist
                and seraph-winged woodsmoke
              nestle into memory's quilts ~
sunstruck blue Pyrénées rise behind
        spined chestnut fruit
            my chill-visible breath
              dews.

journal - 9/21/06

the feeling that i can have an effect when my body unbinds and returns elementally to the earth was present throughout the day.

woke at 3H for renal relief and the BELL of Lacommande RANG the 1/2 hour at 3:30H and every hour and half hour there-after... not to mention the clamoring carillon at 7H. i don't get it. anyone who needs to know it's 4H should have a watch. ate my risotto remains and headed out.

amber aureoled cloud sunrise above, and the Pyrénées are a now constant rocky blue presence through the sight-sifting interlace of trees. passed through only one small community, le-Haut-d'Estialescq... dogs, one burnt out house. another of those vicious winged-tick creatures from The Bestiary landed on my right arm, where it died. kersplat.

got to the Oloron Office de Tourisme a few minutes before they closed at noon. the intended gîte - closed. two other options open. first - not back 'til 18:30H. screw that. the other... no answer.

before heading to a cheap hotel i checked out a slim-chance option on rue Revol which the OT's list indicated stopped renting rooms after mid-September... knocked, nothing - left. then the door creaked open. a woman standing there in edenic sunlight. she said they didn't have effectual heating, thus the schedule. but since the weather is so warm - no problem! to please come in.

my hosts bought this 1600's house a few years ago and are slowly renovating it. Pierre is a get-back-to-basics soul... the world moves so quickly let's move 'contre-sens' ...against the grain and with the old stones. he works as a local gardener and refurbishes the house when he can... offering extra rooms to pilgrims, to people on bike or on foot, people who parallel his interests in slowing down and appreciating. questioning. (Are you sure?) holding and considering a pre-purchase... do i need this? is this necessary? is there a place where you can't hear motors? a glance to the reticular contrailed sky.

couldn't help it. undressing for my shower i ripped that toenail right off. tore that mouldering thing off and tossed it in the trashcan after considering taping it to a journal page like Jeff Goldblum's 'Fly,' collecting all the remnants of physical humanity falling from his body and shelving them in the medicine cabinet.

wrung and hung my clothes to dry in the overgrown gardens out back. absorbed in my wringing, a cat came to visit and be stroked... red beetles scuttling by we both ignored.

on my way to the Notre Dame Cathedral i crossed the couple who, out biking, visited Lacommande while i was sketching it... at the time i was preoccupied and oblivious. 'We saw you yesterday!' and we had a genial chat strolling their grandson in a pram. churches in Southwest France are so colored... completely painted interiorly in purples, dark blues, mauves, dark greens, with silver elaborations and highlighting gold paint strokes. when sunlight shines through the stained glass the depth of design and contrast combines in mellow pulsing, sparkling, otherworldly surrounds... walls of watery lights.

Oloron - oddly, a conglomeration of what seems to have been three village centers, which grew together through time. architecture has changed again. stone facades are cinereously monotone in color under steep witch-cap black slate roofs... dramatic with the cataract-carved mountains behind. a 'lifted from a fairy tale' feel...

watching the torrent down below the bridge... thoughts drifting to Anne Hébert and the Shatterer of Worlds - Ivan appears! we caught up for a while. he didn't care for Frike. she had a northern gung-ho-ness that ruffled his southern sensibilities, i think. and i would never have picked up on this but he says Didier used ways - grammar-wise - to keep him at a distance, to avoid using vous / tu forms, and even avoided learning his name. iconoclastic old-boned and blistered man.

9/21/2006

trailside slug in mortal rapture
    writhing segmented
        rust-red skin
  finding some squatted beast's
    fruit-seed speckled
        dung-drop
    in the overarching oak limbs' daylong shade...
      bellys up, hunkers down,
        and feasts to
      starlight-deep contentment.

9/21/2006

between my right hand's walking-staff clasped fingers
    and the chestnut rolling left,
a height-of-the-land warm breeze
    blows round morning flesh soothingly,
        more soothingly than in still chilled low dales.
this much closer to the sky,
    churning cloud bellys
        slowly open eddy-eyes.
my knotted mesh of life burls and unbinds in kind,
    tangles and unwinds ~
to add tenderness to tomorrow's
    quince,
    think it drinking today's tea
        in peaceful present praise.

9/21/2006

4:30 morning church bell clangs.
    valley roosters and subconscious mind riot for
        a while ~
fearing where i'll be
    when my Mother dies,
that tender tie to living
        flickered out.

journal - 9/22/06

for recent mountain storms, the river running through Oloron was raging viscous thick with mud. went to the open market up the other side of the bridge... fish, sausages, curry spice fritters, leathery smells, smells of warm cheese and raw meat. got phonetically confused between 'c'est pareille' and 'séparé.' mailed out film rolls and five bags of Arlequins. i'm hooked on that sweet and sour candy!

up to the hilltop Église Sainte Croix... impressive views of the black-slate city roofs below and mountains beyond. fall air... warm in the sun, cool in the shade. called ahead to reserve a bed.

drew the Cathedral - screwed it up and went back to see my hosts. Cécile is an artist and combines her own paints out of powders. she makes icons in the Russian / Byzantine style and copies of medieval paintings on parchment. amazing... the princess in green forest with a white deer beside the stream, both with royally slender long necks. Pierre gave me a tour through the basement rooms he's been working on which will eventually be a pilgrim's dorm. there's a grand stone fireplace in the reading room corner. and through the wall he broke through and rebuilt is a former shop space that will be her 'atelier' one day... an antique penny-farthing wheeled bike in the window... time opaqued glass golden light.

mellow winters here he says. 20° in February... 20x2=40-4=36+32=68F!

journal - 9/23/06

hearing me in the early morning Pierre got boxers and bare feet up to escort me to the door, wished me well and i set out again through the amber streetlight lit haze. over the thrashing river slowly clearing from mountain silt to mountain clear... to Place Saint Pierre... a bright grocery open... shelves of semi-precious-gem jam jars shine.

followed a narrow lane out into dawn light... the crest ridge trail winding through fields among a tightening scatter of steep cone-like mountainettes... hill and escarpments radiating green.

the field-plains after Lurbe-Saint-Christau... idyllic. a stonewalled cart-track defines pasture from forest, red Autumn ivy seething up gnarly trunked oaks. a couple cars pass me on the narrow lane, couple cars stop... gunshots loudly from the bridge my dewy footsteps are still printed upon. wondering what they shot and had it watched me? now in quick memory's dying eyes.

the crumbling beauty of a ruined stone house under an urchin-packed chestnut tree with the overcast blue mountains behind.

right of the River Aspe. left of the River Aspe. right of the torrential Aspe... a Superlative-ridden trail! a narrow boxwood-grown tunnel shimmering a billion hints and hues of green... sometimes clung high against the mountainside, sometimes following the rain swollen khaki-brown muddy torrent churning thick and powerful from down out the mountains. this thrashing Gave d'Aspe, this constantly thrashing Gave d'Aspe... the mountain storms, mountain heights, mountainside narrow trail... steep wooded escarpments falling away... the sound of the rushing river, the pungent boxwood scent... feeling i could ramble a lifetime of trails like these!

green mountains going white to vanish in the oncoming sheets of rain.

i think the joke is 'nice day if it doesn't rain.' Bedous would be a gorgeous town if the rain stopped and low clouds cleared. but even in obfuscation i can tell it's an impressive locale. i got cloud-broke glimpses of jagged crests towering beyond... closer than beyond... just behind the buildings on the square.

an unplugged fair sprawls across the main square where the gîte facades - kiddie rides wrapped in plastic tarps, their thousands of lights unlit and carnival music quiet... though quite a crowd is seated at long tables eating and drinking under the arcades.

a many-roomed, -corridored and -leveled gîte. no idea what the building was in its youth... the downstairs crammed with municipal junk. made my ablutions and took a nap. drunk guy across the alley singing Aznavour back to the radio. watched rain fall on slate roofs for a while then, emboldened by ennui, went out to wetly explore. found an open bar and a Casino grocery across the street. the bartender's a Brit... laughingly she said the weather forecast for tomorrow is sunny, cloudy, and rainy. Aussie-rules football brutalizing the tube...

9/23/2006

river sounds,
    thick boxwood walled and pungent
        trail making
     a marvel of now ~
forgotten saw-hewn
   mossy black log
     drips
     with
   the wide mountainside's coalescent dew.
one   one   one dew concentrate pearl
      drops ~
    numina so fleet a sphere.

9/23/2006

chill green tomatoes
    on staked wither-vines ~
      after Thursday's torrentials
    Saturday's river runs
crystal rock bottom clear again ~
    mountain air
      and mountain earth
   on the move
    in these late September
     days.

9/23/2006

birdsong manure roses and
    roosters weave
  Oloron-Sainte-Marie behind ~
    now, hill high bovine shapes
      against a blue and fire-coal
        dawn...
    calf-head silhouette
      buried in the udder
        tugs on a silhouette teat...
      the valley swells with nursing's lows ~
watching from a chestnut-burr strewn trail,
  a something pricks the tender skin
    behind my knee
to quaff one warm
    blood drop...
    to quaff a drop of blood
      in the Pyrénées' shadows, whose majestic presence
    i behold, contemplate, and treasure for
the loathsome winged-fang bastard
    my dust
      will sure become.

9/23/2006

  rain sodden boxwood pungent
    tunnel trail,
      the toweringly near mountain horizon
        crests above ~
river invisible but
  to the spirit loud,
    cleansing the vicious and voices
      what cackle man's mind...
      man's would-be moonlight clear ears...
washing with the shifting worldwide shore-sand
    sounds of yesterday's ravined rain
      now surging
        now swelling
    these great gift rift open mountain veins.

9/23/2006

hawk dalliance cries,
  tumbling flight,
    gasped breath and wing-wind recaptured
to soar away o'er liquid green Aspe Valley plains ~

      *

elemental earthen spine
  broke through the mantle crust
    an eon ago
  forms jagged tor lines
    against a mist thick sky.

journal - 9/24/06

the Brit bartender could not have been more right... a day of sun! clouds! rain! clouds and showers mainly. found out, after the fact, that if i had continued on through Urdos a bit there was a 10E gîte ahead. o well. this last night in France can be in an inn with a demi-pension.

now, last night... what the hell was that!? puts a whole new twist on "acceuil chaleureux!" a 'warm welcome' has never been so warm! after the bar, (and the short French whiskey shot), i stocked up at the Casino and went back to cook away the raw air. as i got the carrots and onions going in butter and oil Ivan comes smiling around the corner commenting on the stove-top aromas he knew i was here by. we hung out... ate my pilgrim lentil stew and he reheated his boxed meal. seemed hesitant to try my food. maybe none of the French like carrots and lentils? after a three hour pause the carnival kicked in again with the force darkening night skies give loud carnival lights and bright sounds...

we drank his wine, and just about bed-time... voices and noises downstairs. thought we were busted - Ivan smoking a butt in the tinder-beam building - but no. the 'responsable' for the gîte came up with a friend... both appreciably lit. and it was all downhill from there. the whiskey bottle they brought, the bloc of hash they brought, the conversations, the laughter at that bedeviled toilet on the constant flush like the raging Gave d'Aspe itself... the laughter after one of my rambling stories when Ivan turns to me and says in French, 'You know you've been speaking English for ten minutes and we have no fucking idea what you're saying!' it was then that Gîte-Man, with his stunted left arm, breaks out the clarinet and starts wailing tunes on it... long, long night.

Gîte-Man and his punk bartender friend took off. Ivan mixed his toxins, got the head spins and went to puke countless times... looking quite greeny-grey last i saw him - and that was the last time i saw him... vanishings between the Chemin and the Starry Way. i got a drunken energy burst and cleaned the gîte - was up until 3H. 3H!! i shall always celebrate 'la fête pour la St. Michel' on 9/23.

awoke hazily. found the boulangerie and grabbed a tresse... fat old man with a black beret in front of me put two baguettes in a threadbare pillowcase and shuffled his way home.

roadside waterfall. crystal water shattering over stone and then flowing away in silence... whole.

and after 4K the tummy rumbles, the twitching sphincter responds. long search for a secluded corner and oh those lentils changing form... transformation's closer than it seems. transfiguration, too. and transubstantiation's all the same in golden, red-votived shrines. the hot brown pile left behind for celebratory slug feasts and tap-root exultations.

a Sunday without gunshots. passed by many crumbling granite train stations left to ruin by the no longer functioning railway. didn't shoot them but i should have as a photographic series on aesthetic disintegration. had to use my staff to press down several 'clôture électrique' lines so's not to shock the inner thigh straddling stonewalls and live wires. those September light purple saffron crocuses are a-bloom diffusely on the trail, sprouting through dark green grasses.

coming down transhumantly, a herd of Pyrénées mountain goats with wool so long it was dragging on the road... shepherds, dogs, and neck bells clanging... swamping cars in a slow avalanche of woolly rolling boulders! perched myself up on a stump for to bide their passage. a kid in an overwhelmed car was hanging his whole torso out the window to pet, poke, and giggle glee among the passing clatter-hooved beasts. afterwards, the fresh goat-shit pebbles made my boot treads useless.

because of brain haze i had no sense of time and it seemed to pass quickly - quickly into Urdos. got in just after 13H. this whole mountain commune is out of power. at some vague point late last night while cleaning, staccato window flashes i took for cameras suddenly thundered! and the power surged and faded several times. must have never made it back on up here. water's barely still warm in the tanks so i showered quickly, then moseyed about... the feeling of having gone to bed at 3H and climbed a mountain slowly filling eyes and mind.

across the gorge from my hotel pillow and window the green mountains engulf more than a third of the sky... minuscule sheep move a scattered slow white progression across an alpine pasture.

passing time with the pen and mind, and flipping through the previous week's newspapers at the bar:

..."La fête pour la Saint Michel commence aujourd'hui" and all those eating under the arcades with wine bottles in scattered lines down long tables... that was the concours d'omelettes puis dégustation! ...an omelette contest? and wine tasting... why not?

...languages mixing - overheard some French using 'borracho' for 'drunk' in Borce. visitor shooting someone's rose garden with a telescopic lens said 'bonjour' to the housewife sweeping who responded 'hola.'

...unnecessary concern for today raised by the warning in the guide. the FFRP didn't mark the trail with red and white bands, (balises), but the Association de Saint Jacques flagged it well with their stylized shells and yellow Voie d'Arles tags.

...heel blisters blooming - i can't believe it. after so many wound-free days. must be from the friction of climbing.

...wonder if pimientos de Padrón will still be available or if they're a seasonal treat? with the hot Spanish south they've gotta have 'em!

...flotsam-stick-n-branch rubble marked many places on the trail today where the flood waters over-reached their bankings. Spanish newspaper says there was much flooding in Jaca and the Aragón Valley as well.

...those people who were at the hotel bar when i arrived at 13:15H are still here for my apéritif, still distractingly loud...

...bellied up to the table. no one's in a rush. the couple who sat a half hour ago hardly have bread and wine...

...and that was a delicious meal. my last meal in France... assiette charcuterie - savory dried sausage, chorizo, prosciutto, two fried calamar rings and greens. soupe de lentilles à l'ancienne. rabbit stew was a treat. the rabbit was roasted, then mushroom and red wine braised and meltingly tender in its gravy. enjoyed the lavender / rosemary flavors of the rabbit back in Arles, but it was tough. a few things have occurred since that meal, it's safe to say... pain, mind, miles, visions and smiles.

i just pulled a goat hair out of my cheese

Aragonia

9/25/2006

grey rock scraped
    alpine meadow green
        crenelate crest tors
pulse morning gold and cloud light.

    *

    each fallen chestnut's
        summer soul
    to timeless stars unbinds

9/25/2006

white mountain fog pillows upon a nameless
    purple petal cuspèd
        saffron stamen sea

9/25/2006

rain cloud...
    now be-diamonded green
        alpine fields flash with 10,000 suns ~

    *

late September gene-triggered
    saffron crocus stamens glow amber-wick-ember anima mundi
        in light purple
            prayer palm petals
    along the rock stumbled trail...
        tucked in ancient boxwood walking
th' invisible river thunders storms

9/25/2006

rain on black slate roof overhang ~
sheer alpine valley meadow
    mountain walls after
        a billion years of Gave d'Aspe erosion ~
white puff cluster dust mote sheep slowly graze
      across one green windowpane

journal - 9/25/06

a day of constant changes. woke up just after 6H despite the wine and was down by 7:30H for petit déj... bread and coffee, two corn muffins and a croissant. the Boozin' Belgian Trio was up and down early as well... less bright of eye, more quiet of tongue. la 'responsable' all-in-one bartender, receptionist, floor 'n pot-scrubber was morningly warmly chattingly friendly in the way good coffee after good rest makes... she wished me well, "courage et chance."

and i headed out through veils of mist-gauzed drizzle that phased on and off all the last remaining 10K of le Chemin d'Arles, which ends upon this mountain's spine in the clouds. only the first four or five K followed the road, then it banged a left up into wooded mountain slopes, shorter and sheerer than the low-saddle-seeking road winds. a steep forest trail narrowly walled in with pungent boxwood, serrate-leafed beech and mossy stones... the infinite hues of green dancing phantoms with the fog. had some stumbling trouble - the body-engine working hard-and-hot in the cool humidity fogged my glasses and depth perception was lost. before clambering up into the clouds, where very little was visible anyway and depth perception mattered not, i got a few shots of Urdos way down below... the nestled town's amber-lit streetlights flickering a constellation against broad V-gorge slopes behind... a gorge rolling full with lightning-veined cumulonimbal boulders.

in the heights the temperature dropped, glasses cleared and alpine fields unfurled. cloudbank boa-ed mountain summits surround sight... tsunami vapor-waves climbing, uncoiling out of cavernous green valleys, on the slow crawl up precipitous mountainsides seeming great underwater beasts grazing coral reefs... slowly, nebulously, consciously creeping. monolithic shadowy shy tors looming their silhouettes then vanishing back into clouds... like feeling the sky-gods pull away after finishing their peering at pismire man.

Somport's Refugio / Bar was open when i arrived at 11H. ordered in Spanish for the first time in a while... the tongue all a-twist between French muscle-memory and the intended Spanish in my mind. had a coffee while watching clouds break into shattered sunlight over Spain, empty chair-lift chairs and cables swinging nearby in the wind. spoke with an older Spanish couple... he's done the Camino from Somport and from various other starting points. after regarding my banged up and oddly bandaged Lomo in his hand for a moment he snapped a picture for me of me by the '858K left to Santiago' waymarker! so many miles gone. so many yet to go. and with bliss in the bloody marrow bones i strode strongly on down the steep rip-rap rocky Camino Aragonés... thoughts of Jack and Japhy galloping down a Matterhorn Peak mountainside, silent skies echo their eternal howl and joy.

kudos to those maintaining the trail! but i must say the visible battle of Camino organizations left me laughing. a Spanish yellow arrow on stump or stone showing the way... then two feet later on stump or stone, a red and white French Grande Randonnée (GR) balise. you guys love your paint! although there's no complaint about a well-marked trail.

but well-marked trail or not, they've got some hefty work to do after these storms... destruction! wreckage! ruination! a waterfall that must have been a rager a day or so ago slammed an immense stump and stump's root-enmeshed flotsam against a cement footbridge in the forest, battering the railings into twisted shrapnel. had to scramble over a boulder-and-scree landslide before the bridge to the N330. and the torrentials flowing off the mountains used the trail itself as a sluiceway, eroding the Camino away completely in places. serious flooding in Canfranc Estación... branch and log debris lodged high in roadside fences and Iwo-Jima-jammed in the saturate roadside earth. an engineer armed with a tightrope walker's long pole paces the dam's catwalk dislodging forestral wrack and clotting limbs from the floodgates.

met a peregrino below the dam. he left his car up at the Somport Refugio... only going as far as Puente la Reina during this week's vacation. he did Puente to Logroño last year... Juan. Juan, who with instinctual generosity, immediately offered me part of his breakfast bar then tossed the shiny wrapper on the ground. yep, back in Spain.

in Somport Pueblo, Canfranc Estación and Canfranc Pueblo there are profusions of six-storey high Marxist grey cement block housing being built... practical, but not in the least attractive.

turning around to view the heights i've come down from - clouds break. mind gasps. titanic vapor waves corkscrew off wet sun-struck-flaring massif ledge faces. snow-fringed alpine meadow bowls glowing green, unreachable Edens i imagine must be a haven for reclusive animals, a micro-climate for that one flower still in existence upon the Earth. at my feet, gale-strewn carmine mountain ash berries and storm-crushed purple crocuses among the ferrous bloodred stones.

came across three poutníci from the Czech Republic... so it was they who made those bootprints in the soft morning mud! they stayed in Jaca last night, bussed up to Somport and started from there early this morning... back to stay in Jaca tonight. Juan too, was headed further on to Jaca. Jim, no. Jim stopped in Villanúa and is dealing with things that are not the way he wants them to be. the gimcrackery pompous ego bruised, wondering why the universe doesn't see things his way. the albergue is closed 15H - 18H... 18H! would have waited but the two bars here are closed and the one still open is closing 16H - 19H! shorter days, cooler temps... 'how is anything hand-washed and hand-wrung going to dry overnight' thoughts... thoughts of morning's clammy socks and Phillip Roth's refrigerated calf liver.

instead of twiddling my thumbs for three hours on a cold park-bench i ended up going to the hostal and spent more than double what patience would have cost but, a room's a room and repose has value - even in this slipshod place. it looks new at first but actually all they've done is a sloppy job of refacing a dingy hotel. 35E? that means a hot earlobe-deep bath to me, man. you can have my cash but i'm working your boiler.

so happy that with all this climbing and descent - no blisters, no abrasions. but for the long trajet down over rocky terrain, the meat is aching among the metatarsals.

undressing... beaming with effusive joy when i remembered i don't have to wash my socks! "ahhh, 'tis the little things!" that second pair i bought in ? long ago were intended for my first full day in Spain... mañana! so no more stitching the Smart Wool's toes. out of respect for the chambermaid i'll bag these sweat-jam-nasty things, but they're going in the trash. man who signed me in said dinner's at 20:30H... 20:30H! yep, back in Spain... and the épicerie, now an alimentacion again, does not open until 17H! yep, back in Spain!

9/25/2006

high over Gave d'Aspe torrent's roar,
    purling pool alpine meadow sheep bells sound
        through silent cloud-boulder landslides ~

*

   slow valley vapor mist pillars rise,
      gauze, creep and glean
         steep mountain forests,
            fumeroling delphicly in effortless serpentines...
   a healer's conscious phantom fingers caress
      crest and ravine,
         massage sedimentary earthen memory
      to the slate and granite root-wrapped riparian spine ~
the ass crack back dimple dripped raindrop chill
      awakens me away from shape-shifting reverie

9/25/2006

boxwood, beechnut fall, a ruin's shag-mossy stone walls,
   wavering fern fronds swim fishbone shadows on the loam...
      ruby mountain-ash berries bead
         with silver pattering rain,
     and the trees sieve reeling phantoms from swathes of fog ~
ancient cart-track to an ancienter pass
      weaves me and mountain
         into Spain

journal - 9/26/06

slept so well with the ravine-coursed winds raging by my window all night long - an ahhh... cleansing sound. desayuno is all wrapped in plastic... plastic-wrapped magdalenas and a pan de leche 'L.A. Confidentially' cut to look like a croissant. back in the land of the 'industrials.' babbling above the bar, Spanish morning TV is as vapid as in the States.

i saw a BOAR! just before Castiello de Jaca - heard gravel crunching, squinted ear and eye to the right and a medium-sized boar was scrambling legs up a schisty hillside... tufts of dark brown forebrow hair, just like a cartoon Pumbaa! at last a boar!

behind the restaurant with a black steel silhouette of a peregrino bending against the wind i wended down to the river described as wide, but not deep, with stepping stones placed for the traverse... and it was raging! forget stepping stones! i had to crab-walk, skootch, balance and butt-slide across cement pilings driven into the riverbed, but i made it... adrenaline twitching fingers and breath. all along the riverbank the long grass was slicked down by storm waters, looking like whorled low-tide kelp. sat down to de-pebble a boot and grinned at a yellow arrow painted on a flood-shifted stone pointing awry into the scrub brush and sky.

considered spending the night in Jaca but it really was too early in the day to stop. arrived by 11:30H with the trail so straight and level lending itself to steady treading rhythms... body felt fantastic - down to the heels even. sat at a café and enjoyed a pastry filled with candied calabacín... went in to lube the crotch as the 'kleine wulfje' was starting to growl. leaving, my footsteps stepped in line with a street corner crowd of Russian tourists... momentary dishevelment in the sudden Cyrillic sea but i outpaced them easily, digital cameras and all.

passed ruined military buildings and barracks with an active shooting range popping echoes off the hillside. heading due west at last along a wide valley-plain nestled between high hills to the south and the Pirineos to the north... some peaks back near Somport flashing snow-white-vein ravines. after a couple rapprochements with the Nationale the trail headed abruptly up to longly skirt a mountainside... boxwood and oak scented. using wind-on-flesh sensations to sustain Present Mind.

saw my first broke-open bag of Spanish trash on a pastoral hillside and wondered what crime environmentalism could be? these people need the ten years of weeping Indian commercials i had in my childhood. true, the White Devil wiped out the Native Populations but in the 70's at least we learned not to dump garbage on the ground.

headed down to the outskirts of Santa-Cilia-de-Jaca where more of those ugly grey Marxist edifices were going up. a facelifted town center... attractive enough, but nothing in particular to say about its stones or roses. my first Americans! Jake and Kiki and their daughter from San Diego. they directed me to the albergue and... whoa! people people everywhere and not a breath to think... nearly full. a Dutch couple - the three Americans - a group of French i didn't see until later on the street.

spotless albergue... rez calzada is a commodious room with sitting space and a small kitchen. two dorms on the second floor. the third floor is all tables and chairs... another dual-usage albergue / community function room.

folks settling into siesta-mode... i took off for a tour about town that quickly ended at this narrow three-tabled bar... bartender with a lazy lolling eye, elderly mom with perfectly set hair, her brawnily haunched daughter skirted by, a red sweatered local with a shuffle shuffles through the room, fucking flies...

the Americans made scrambled eggs and salad and were half done wolfing down their plates before my onions were even golden. lentil stew reverie. the Dutch couple is bussing back to Jaca for money... no magic cash-from-a-wall machine here. the French octet doing the trail with relay cars, some walking - 'tele-grinos,' 'peregrinos-lite' - were slowly amassing and loud. the sardonic asides, cognomens and epithets bestowed upon those hiking the trail with a puny humpback-daypack and an air-conditioned coach providing luggage portage and a lift to the noon lunch spot, if one is lagging, are many. as an object of meditation i've said many times, "Everyone has their own Camino." ...everyone has their own path... to each their own way. but i find no internal patience for their pussified aches and lames.

the hospitalera came by for sellos and payment - a rabidly chatty character was she. sweet, chubby, helpful - offering towels and washing machine usage. she spent the day in front of the TV and had a splitter of a headache. didn't seem to keep her from talking - or maybe it did? i don't know her norms. but i imagine moving any faster her lips would spark.

then the night went weird! the dark streets and bare-bulb bar were suddenly a-swarm with retiree Brits heading to upper rooms the bar must let. one old Brit, a Finn, a Swede, a Czech all flew down from England to the provincial airstrip nearby, on their way to southern Spain to meet their wives... BAM! a peregrino pack coming in at 21H comprised, in part, of the Jaca Czech trio and three Spanish women... what?! how long have they been stumbling through the penumbra? Kiki is a bit of an organizer. (euphemism.) she came looking for me and my minimal Spanish to search out where Chubby Migraine lived so the new crew could be checked in, and i'm thinking 'if she's not here and they're all sleeping on the floor anyway the night's free. big deal.' clearly the Spanish could care less, but the egalitarian American needed to ensure each peregrino payed.

journal - 9/27/06

i was first to rise and many soon followed. the Jaca Czechs who slept on couches downstairs, the refinanced Dutch couple, Americanos - all up salving feet and thighs, calves, corns, and crotches... snipping gauze and taping it to appendáges. looked like a goddamned M*A*S*H triage. the one tall dark-complected woman, the one with a seriously fatigued and frustrated face, she was first to leave without a wave or nod at 6:30H. she wore the same face last night. the lot of them took the wrong and extremely long trail, thus their late arrival and collective tortured mien.

left in the just lightening darkness. exposed Pirineos' crests phasing from light grey to gold with the rising sun. from a deep morning chill and frozen fingers thawing, to sunny dry hot-oven breezes...

a white gravel trail winding through blond wheats, bankings of red rosehip coals, and rustling poplar groves, to lunar landscapes of what my French guide is calling 'marne bleu' ...a blue marl - enormous blue-grey outcroppings of erosion sculpted mudstone looking like gargantuan mythical beast paws poised on a crevasse ledge, ready to pull the gargantuan mythical beast itself out from the depths behind.

a dragon-faced apparition blossoms out of cirrus clouds above... the whitewashed village of Berdún wedding cakes a hilltop distance off to the north... the litany of rusty-rock hillside communities to the south with their turreted square-towered churches. cocoa golden and amber plumed hawks - one in wide-winged slowly circling flight... another diving with W-angled wings comes whipping down skimming talon-knuckles across the tilled burnt-sienna earth. stopping steps, i could hear her feathers ripping through the air - a heart swelling sound.

mountainside excavation? dynamite blasts from across the reservoir and their landslide-long echoes fissure lyric mind.

again - quick time to Ruesta - flat rhythms - made 35K in 7.5 hours.. a gaunt Spanish / American arrived. he's heading in the other direction towards Rome. Juan of the Canfranc dam showed up with the frustrated-faced woman from last night, plus two other señoras in their 50's. most of today's walkers stayed in Arrés. most who stayed in Arrés must have gotten word that Ruesta is in complete ruins - entirely caved-in but for the albergue - but scaffolding, bulldozer, and masonry work is being done. the revitalizing quality of the Camino is not just for the individual pilgrim. that this rubble is coming to life again as an outpost on the way to Santiago is nothing but positive. just dig up some saint's ulna and a blood-crusted miracle and they've got it made!

the Spanish / American peregrino is following a spare regimen - important for him to know what's available to eat growing on the way... fruits, nuts, whatever the gleaners have left behind. not sure if he's on a raw food diet or choosing to survive on found foods, but he looked pallid and emaciate to me and i question the sense of the practice while on an exacting trail - but whatever... and the sky is blue. initially i want to paraphrase a friend who has no patience with a waif's waist-line and say, "That guy needs a ham and butter sandwich," but i respect the internal trail that he is perceptibly enjoying.

as there is neither an active gas conduit nor propane tank deliveries to the albergue, i guess i'm waiting until 20:30H for the menú to be served.

together we lately ate rice-filled morcilla, fried pork loin with a béchamel, and fried peppers. Juan of the Canfranc dam, the two women are from Logroño, Magdalena, whose face had softened... and a young hospitalero in training from Argentina autodidactically working on his English. while we practiced the phonetics of - tip... chip... cheap... the stars and Milky Way were unutterably amazing in the lightless rural night.

9/27/2006
pre-dawn chill dark blue light,
    journeying west again...
long serrate finger leaves graze cheek and
    knuckle-cracking bootstep sounds...
  the late September chestnut tree
    recognizes man.
glasses fog stopping,
trail pebbles' dew-stippled eastern facets
  shine a shattered iris,
    ceaseless mind

9/27/2006

popcorn crunch beneath
   a thick boot sole ~
      oops, ..., crap.
  another trail snail
     in integrate disintegration
       inches toward nirvana

9/27/2006

weerdly   wierdly   weirdly
   atop the green hillcrest, standing,
    one white horse
   - dots -
  against an all blue sky,
    one jet contrail
      exclamation
       (!)

     *

leafless end-September rugosa
    trailside bramble
       in firecoal rose-hip
        profusion ~
stigmata swelling upon thorny branches,
   treading the nowhere on Earth Shakyamuni has not wept

     *

long white gravel trail
    barely bends to wend through
  cocoa-golden tilled field rows,
     waiting for what seeds may Springtime come...
now receiving raptor beak cast bone,
   songbird song,
     my time alone

*

on tractor-churned earth phasing shades
    from bull-blood dark mud
        to sun and wind dried dusty rose,
grand tuft-thighed eagles
    leave handspan wide talon prints,
    take slow silent flight,
        reign th' eternal blue
            between mountain and the night

9/27/2006

little medieval village of Berdún
    cake tiers
the river-eroding Spanish plain,
        blue Pirineos' foothills roll away to jagged tors
        behind,
white jet vapor trails railroad tie
    feet, eyes, and mind to north-face
        French memories
    beneath this still blue sky

9/27/2006

on one weathered silver stubble field
    two motionless crows
        in tilt-head pearl black eye to eye
            silent conversation ~
while green forested mountain crests break
    into grey-gold-rust rock sedimentary
        striations,
    the slow earthen mantle tide crashes
        upon millennial plains

journal - 9/28/06

woke up dreaming of my half-prodigal cat Terrapin. he vanished - i'm hoping for the happy return for to crack ope a tin of gravied veal.

left by 7:30H and another day of changes passed, but with an unsettling sense of timelessness.

descended steeply down from the Ruesta ruins through a deserted campground, a burnt-out caravan churning mafia imaginations... over a long plank bridge to a clement wood-road... through a glen where pilgrims have balanced hundreds of rock pile cairns - a mystical fairy-ville enclave. a clement wood-road longly rising to the crest to finally look out over expansive valley-plains.

had the red carpet rolled out for me in a way better than any Cathedral could. far ahead, a beater of a car followed by a slow moving tractor advanced up the hard-packed, mud rutty track. approaching, the old man driving the car laughed his hello. steering the tractor's buffed steel blade, his son plows seasonal erosion's craters and furrows into smoothness... and i had the honor of stepping the first! the first down the dark red earthen track, stepping into the day ceremonious.

my footfalls following the cobbled Roman road... a flock of fifty storks whirlwind up to black-speck heights above the Aragón River. and like splay-fingered miniature men, frogs leap into muddy rainwater 'ponds' at my approach, making me grin... kick another ripple in the Tao.

crossed the border into Navarra after Undués de Lerda. saw Sangüesa from a hilltop just before noon, but it felt more like just after 15H. familiar foul smell on the wind. reading ahead in the guide... tomorrow morning i pass by a paper mill.

walking down one metallically clattering street - odd - there seem to be an inordinate amount of seniors with canes, and crutches clasped to forearms wandering about... a retirement home nearby, of course, but it felt like running an agèd Gauntlet! i wonder if Clint Eastwood is dumping in a diaper yet? went to Municipal Offices for the albergue key and the sello. paid a no-nonsense man who stamped stamp and stamped date, stamping copies stamping shuffling stamping rustling and stamping... a perfect 1950's small town clerk-bureaucrat caricatured.

no one from this trail family is here at the albergue yet. i think most of them are ending this year's leg of the Camino at Puente la Reina, and since they're not going further they're serpentining off and on the Camino doing a loose monastery tour. i'm content to walk the line along the daylong chain of square-towered Romanesque churches, often placed strategically for defense at the town or river's edge. when the one-time Dukes of Aragón and Navarra financed church construction - they got a fortress! à bon chat, bon rat.

odd bar - South American run, i think, for their high Aztec cheekbones. red Asian paper light globes hang golden tassels and buoy in the breeze... on the walls, vintage red, white and blue French placard ads for Butil Frères butter and Farine Lactée - a folded newspaper tricorne-wearing blond girl tasting the blissful cream of wheat from her fingertip.

it's HERE! it's here! good Lordy in late September it's here! several days before limping into Salamanca back in July, a journalist from 'Grandes Espacios,' Spain's outdoor magazine, photographed me hiking. he'd run ahead and shoot as i approached, run ahead and shoot. said the photos may appear in the September issue. and Sangüesa being the first place in Spain, (since i remembered that event), populous enough to support a newspaper / stationary shop... in my fumbled Spanish i described the type of magazine to the counter-clerk. 'Oh, this one?' he asked, slipping a revista out from the layered jumble. and in a pre-perceptive flash i recognized the colors of the clothes i've worn and washed for four months...

"Sí!! That's ME!" and i'm on the freakin' cover! with a full-page spread inside as well! what a riot!

the gene that does such things alive and a-thrive in my Mother's heart... it was a mere matter of days before the cover image was all over the internet and copies bought and framed. she doesn't speak a word of Spanish but i doubt China's still-standing Great Wall ever met a mother's will!

9/28/2006

from powder blue
    to hearth-ember amber
        glows a morning trail,
  winding ahead through the gloaming ~
seen from this side of the horizon's fulcrum,
    high-angled dawn-warm sun rays settle to
        compress a chill
            upon the earth,
  upon the last of forest shrouded night,
        sieving birdsong
            into today's first madrigal cloud spray

9/28/2006

low valley plain bowling
    sunlight and birdsong refrains,
  cool late-September wind
    on warm skin walking west ~
one long Summer's effort
    heat and rain wheat stalk
        my tongue rolls along the roof-ridge,
            rudders between teeth and cheek
like St. Francis in 1214 walking to Compostela
        keeping his own mouth moist...
    old tricks of journeyed days
        alive in younger bones and eyes

journal - 9/29/06

Monreal... "no T! no T!" the rule-regulation-edict-obsessed German said looking over his glasses and shaking his finger at me this morning (...wichser...) is the type of renovated town all the others want to emulate. up-to-date inside, old stone without, quiet cobblestone streets and flowering windowbox cascades. from an oak and pungent boxwood forest i slipped in this afternoon across a skewed medieval dos d'âne bridge, oddly downward-dogging over a reedy stream.

after all these miles it's still a bizarre perception to me... i hike in on a meandering trail to the field-side of town, and unbeknownst on the other side a major roadway passes by! and this bar is a truck-stop with a dust-muted disco ball and brazen one-armed-bandits bubbling notes, dropping electronic cataracts of falling-coin sounds.

the Edict of Worms isn't here. he must have continued 13K on to the next albergue. he, or rather my exchange with him this morning, polluted my mind throughout the day... 'flies in front of the eyes or flies behind them.' he sneeringly rated my guide 'OK' - probably because it was French... and was adamant about the Compede. he got visibly angry when i voiced my criticism of the dressing and went off loudly on how i was applying it wrong. i stopped listening long before he stopped talking. he did the Vía de la Plata this spring. a few years ago he trekked from Le Puy... at one point through five days straight of rain. the last day of the deluge he stayed in a hotel with a wide blazing fireplace and a maternal caretaker who kept feeding him gentiane jaune. i tried to keep that cozy image of him in the fore instead of the story of his agreeing outright with the ego-ridden priest in Santiago who told the congregation to turn off their cellphones, and when three later rang - with piaffe and splutter he stormed out of the Cathedral! if the holy mass and sacraments therein are so bloody special get over yourself in your brocaded robes and golden palace that Almighty-Precious-Thee were not obeyed.

the Edict of Worms generously shared his wine last night and his snoring this morning. between he and Juan rumbling on i didn't sleep much after 4H. got up, reheated me lentil stew and left in the dark. looped around the vaporously sparkling paper mill, up to Rocaforte and past St Francis' fountain. dwelling on history and the objects and actions in time... Francis made the pilgrimage from Rome to Santiago in 1214 and left one of his older monks here to found a monastery. the fountain still flows though man's walls have crumbled.

a steep climb to the crest overlooking low hill-ranged-in plains... rising, rising... an open wood road... up and up and... up. and at a bifurcation... no balise... no flecha - uh oh. there's always an indication at a fork or bend. and when was the last time i actually saw a yellow arrow? ...uh oh.

well down the mountain the actual Camino dog-legged off to the right on a narrow goat track that wound hills, scrub forests and rolling horse pasturelands dissevered by heavy gates to slide-bolt-open and slide-bolt-close.

bright-tined and bright-bladed combines and threshers pose with the untameable mountains behind. tilled varicolored croplands counterpaned against hill and plain, pulse with patterned cloud light. one articulate hawk sculls evenly away over it all into black mote and vanish. foot flesh aches. 35K with my mistake today. 31K tomorrow.

interesting conversation with Magdalena before the others arrived. she said there's a story from this region of a monk who went out for a wandering walk, listening to the birds... and he came back 350 years later! (wondering on the Rip Van Winkle theme through literary history... the Seven Sleepers of Ephesus, et al.) timewise, she had the odd experience of never seeming to reach the San

Javier monastery, thus her late arrival in Santa-Cilia. and being unaware of either her experience or the fable... my odd time-shift sensation entering Sangüesa. a temporally warped area perhaps? a vortex? rivers, mountains... who knows? that experience was doubled today. after i started back down the wood-road looking for arrows i could not flippin' believe how far i climbed without seeing any. no way was the ascent as long as the descent - no way. witchcraft and vortices.

a cumulative weariness of travel is invading me... fatigue collecting in the spiritual marrow. having a hard time understanding Juan and the Logroñas. usually i get the gist but i just don't understand what they're saying. with this tiredness comes impatience and with impatience i just want to go to a bar / café and not have accursèd flies crawling on my legs and nape... just once! no flies! yo Yahweh! the flies! enough!

a stroll to the sparely stocked grocery. bought a hunk of tortilla at the bar and the last baguette in the bread shop. made a salad, a bocadillo, and shared with the troops. they shared their wine, cheese and chorizo - eventually, that is! i observed an odd cultural clinging. not a one of them could eat the cheese or chorizo they plated and put out without bread! they sat around and stared at the platter as if it were pauper-longing-for-more empty! a habit became a physical impossibility and Juan ran out - literally - to knock on doors like a mad bread begging mendicant... gone for at least a half hour before coming back in with a loaf of day-old.

9/29/2006

foot crushed fig fall,
    fermentation's sour scent
and drunken bees collide stone walls
    falling on their backs,
  buzzing furious at
    the overturned sky

twig, leaf and brush burnt in barrels'
    particular scent
        a city seldom knows

~

Monreal's white stucco walls,
   red geraniums bloom
      in pots wrought-iron-clutched
         to wrought-iron-barred
 windows and balcony grates

~

waiting for the alimentacion to open,
   all muscles that 35K contracted
       me here ache
      meat to the core...
 a bocadillo, bottle of musty home-brew wine and a bed is
    my waking dream

9/29/2006

papermill smokestacks fumeroling
    water ballet
  synchronisms with the still and the breeze, the still and the
      breeze
    above pearl bright
      floodlights lining
   factory building seams.
sweat damp around
  collar 'n nape for the steep climb
    by St. Francis' fountain,
     charred marshmallow scent,
       grease-stained stone picnic table,
         rusted iron firepit grill...
miracle staff-struck fountain
    from the mountain flows still.
   little flower stories stuck in melting time

9/29/2006

hat brim useless,
  blinding white gravel track
    field-fringed with silver wild hays
     untouched by threshing
       tractor tines ~
tilled earthen rows ripple away
    to tree-bristled
      mountain crests
     belly-tickling the swim of clouds ~
a special light shines the blue bowl sky
    and there is no end to cricket listening

journal - 9/30/06

Magdalena left first... we four next... Juan and i soon outpaced the

Logroñas as the cloudy warm morning started to rain. a drenching rain... then Juan fell behind.

as it has done almost all week, the due-west trail ribboned along the open and tree-hugged hillsides to the south. for the moisture those Metta black flies throve! ease of mind, ease of mind, ease of mind not so easily succeeds. and suddenly more explosions! a whole mountainside shorn away by two stone-crushing quarry operations whose dust got in my eyes, blackening teeth and spit.

trailed out into grapevines... a couple tunnels under a couple empty highways... nicked a couple villages... Tiebas was the intended café-stop but nothing there was open... lone sing-songy girl on a pink-tasseled bike back-and-forthing away the time lent a Twilight Zone atmosphere to the quiet day.

in the fields - a color faded but fragrance-full row of lavender. i picked a sprig to stick in my sweat-soured shoulder strap.

craned my neck through the open bakery window in Eneriz looking for pastry - nada. broke through rattling rainstick sounding fly-bead strings into the bar for a Bitter Kas. legs sore. Spanish crew of peregrinos who trod road instead of trail clattered oddly past, as if soled with taps. they were followed oddly by a kid with a mullet cut (exactly like his dad's) rumbling on a Big Wheel. heading out after the break the dirt road was strewn with mealy gold-kernel crushed ears of corn.

surrounded by deep-rilled grapevines and eroded fallow tillage is the XIIth Century Romanesque Santa Maria de Eunate, which is architecturally based on the Church of the Holy Sepulchre in Jerusalem. a lot of talk about the 'energy' there. encircled with arcades, it's pretty enough outside. inside, it was full of a frustrating Spanish trait - of standing in a church a foot away from a conspicuous placard stating in seven languages that 'This is a place of prayer and meditation. Please respect the silence.' ...and hollering to the person they're beside. that's Eunate to me.

what struck me leaving was the rich birdsong in the trees.

the 30th! and i'm in Puente la Reina again, fumbling with the final tattered page of my Chemin d'Arles guide. it has brought me quite some way, this guide... nostalgia's sighs... the final tattered page.

this is a new Camino - Arles is over, Aragonés is now over. this is the Camino Francés and not the 2004 summertime trail. from now on all will be seen in the curious light of repeating something totally new... like ghostly encountering déjà-vu in a different mind.

checked into the refugio and the hospitalero put me in a 10-bedded dorm with an American family who has, so far, not much to say.

peculiar open market in a deserted stretch of fairgrounds... crimson piles on the dusty ochre ground... at least ten wind-flapped tents selling ONLY red peppers! for fire-roasted piquillo or smokey pimentón, he wonders?

a lot of fresh faces, untempered bloody feet and aching thighs - peregrinos starting from Roncesvailles or Pamplona, a mere few days upon the trail.

back at the albergue, the Camino family crumbles. the Logroñas were outside with their husbands and daughters festively hugging, ending this stage, packing still nearly new backpacks in the back of their cars. Juan is going to a Logroña's house tonight, then bussing back to the car he left up at the Somport Refugio. Magdalena gave me a sweet hug and a sweet note saying i had restored her faith in North Americans. peyots shaking, hands and eyes to sky... such power, who knew i had?!

they think they're picking me up at the albergue in Logroño and that i'm staying the night with them, but i'm realizing now i screwed up on the serious side. mind full of 'what next?' and 'what if?' crap. back in Sarlat i miscounted the math between the etapas from Puente la Reina to Santiago and my remaining time in Spain. since then that second guide has been deep beyond daily reference in the pack. counting now... aside from one day of rest pillowed on in León, i'll be having to undertake a slew of 38-40K days across the whole north of Spain in order to make it to Santiago on the 25th. merde. i miscounted the math and must press on but i should leave them a note on the albergue door.

saw the Italiana with groceries and questioned her. there was an alimentacion open on Saturday afternoon! bought a lot out of glee. too much, but i have feastings for tonight and tomorrow. made a thick-stacked chorizo, onion, tomato and tortilla bocadillo that boggled the minds of two Australian couples in the albergue's dining hall. and the reticent cycling Americans opened up - especially the kid. they're from Sacramento. i told him he looked exactly like Nick from '8 is Enough' and he glazed over in a fog of incomprehension the way kids do... had no idea what i was talking about.

familiar pain in the right foot's big toe... another blister beneath the nail. Aussies drinking wine and playing cards. fat drunk dirty Frenchman slur-rambling against a wall i think he's hearing responses from.

broken water, spanish rain

Puente la Reina - Estella

a Norse couple in their early 20's down at breakfast... they boiled a pot of rice with powdered milk and covered the mound with sliced apples and bananas... people who know how to sustain the body! got a fair palmera at the pastry shop and followed the long amber-lit stone canyon street down through Puente to her eponymous bridge.

a soft foggy-fielded morning... lightheartedness swelling. a German trio. two kept stopping to kiss... the same two, at least for today. a day of elative déjà-vu. blaze-white hillcrested Cirauqui appears risingly over the red-earthed vine rows like a towering African savannah termite mound... tunneled, darkly arcaded and close winding shadow-draped streets... the rubble stone steps vertiginously leading down out the back of the village. stopped for a sip in Lorca at one of two dueling 'cross-the-street bars. this guy's had the place for three years. he asked if i had learned Spanish in South America... wonder what i said or how?

Villatuerta Villatuerta Villatuerta. telescoping time. 2004 memories of meeting an Austrian pilgrim in France who recounted his overnight mountain crossing one evening... a story that prompted me to my own adventure of traversing the midnight and hot wind-blasted Pyrénées in full white moonlight going pearl, bone, yellow, golden, orange, then horizonly magnified - setting blood-red over Spain... dawn's sunrise among mountain peaks... eagles peal and soar. memories of suddenly bumping into him weeks later in Villatuerta. i blessed him for his tales.

picture perfect postcard shot of Estella's lofty dos d'âne bridge, the hilltop church behind and rippling blue curtain skies. went to the smaller private albergue i remembered off the main drag... neighbors hanging out the fifth floor window shouting down to me that it has closed for the season! and the rest of town is zipped up Sunday-tight. fiestas were rocking the cobblestones last time i was here and i recall resenting the 22H albergue curfew.

hospitalero checking us in at the municipal albergue was pretty harsh with the French kid from Moissac, hobbling on his infected blister. the guy's just asking about busses. you're working at an international albergue, buddy, not everybody speaks Spanish. from the desk drawer he pulled out a warm can of San Miguel for a full-throated swig.

this small 18-bunk-arrayed room is fitting in the whole crew... four Aussies, French Blister Boy, an older Frenchman i'd relayed with throughout the day, Grocery-Italiana asleep with the sleeping bag over her head because there was a breeze and her hair was wet - what? ...it's 75°!?

out the albergue front door there's a bench across the flagstoned street that in perpetual performance-art fashion pedestals stiff-muscled peregrinos tending feet in robotic staccato motions.

made a risotto sautéing onion, carrots, garlic... then rice, water, tomato and yesterday's chorizo, thyme and trailside fennel... added fridge-foraged leftover parmesan and a few cherry tomatoes. the dried hot peppers in the cupboard i'm going to pilfe... a splash of red wine vinegar. mmm.

I

Puente la Reina albergue,
    strangers bunk-stacked
        and bedded in a restless room,
            rain falls by open windows...
some pilgrims, like with a loose tooth or toenail, worry worry on
                tomorrow's trail,
some just listen to the rain.
    breathing deepens
        whispers 'round
            glottis and nostrils,
crescendo-ing in bang-pipe schoolhouse boiler
    reverberations that
        strangely background dream

II

blue morning cypresses are faint
    in river vapour veils,
        rooster crows rise
            and medieval stone bridge footsteps slow, then still...
sniffing a fistful of trailside gleaned green fennel seeds,
    the dark lightens.
        and though i've never seen their blossoms
            black olives bead dew-shimmering leaves...
a man a-shine in crimson rosehip light

III

climbing high and steeply through valley mist
    to be suddenly ablaze in low-sun angled rays...
        sweat streams trickle the
            body entirely tickling skin
        giggling in
            morning light

IV

a pebble, goat-shit and grass patched
    trail winds
        through gorse heather heath enveloped
            hillsides...
        he learns to send
    spirit out the way
the snail unspirals
    antennae and tail

Estella - Viana

seemed to rest more than sleep... first time in four months i got the top bunk and was narrowly nervous. as quietly as possible i hauled sleepsacksstuffsacksbackpack out of the room to pack. gnawed fruit. not interested in the plastic wrapped breakfast or borborygmasly moaning automat's hot chocolate.

left at 6:40H - knew the way. similar quiet amber-lit stone canyon streets as through Puente la Reina - out through morning 'burbs. a cat vanishes through a paneless black window frame.

winding through hillside young pines... winding through hillside young pines... then on kneeling knees, from cupped hands i sip aubade draughts of wine from the ever-flowing Fuente de Vino behind the Monasterio de Irache Winery - a glowing morning buzz. "Wine is the Blood of the Pilgrim" refrains. trail seemed familiar for a while, out through hillsides of mature oak and pines with grey-stone-crested mountains beyond. then? maybe it was that looking-glass wine. the arrows were there, but? just another time of blurred distortion between trail and guide.

the long serpentining path and tilled rust-red-earthen furrow rows form focal lines that converge and vanish in the blue mountains far ahead.

beyond Los Arcos extend the hot rolling fields, grapevines and olive groves where i once searched the pre-dawn sky for Pleiades meteors. saw the sharp juke right i missed back then, causing me to wander aimlessly long in the star-rent darkness before finding my way. tight-walled and spired Sansol tops the hill ahead.

Torres del Río. met a Belgian woman by the yellow signed tienda and vacillated about staying there at the albergue with her. she, a Québecois couple, and the couple with the donkey lodged in Villamayor de Monjardin last night... shared their scraps into a Jesus-feast and sang watching last night's stars. la Belge likes to tarry and retire at mid-points in the etapas... away from where the crowds tend to stay. while talking with her in Torres... a group of grizzled trouble-making geezers drinking beers on a bench. one's wife called his cell. 'Oh! No! I'm visiting Juan!' and he passes the phone to Juan as proof he's not at the bar... the liquidly beer snarfed repression of laughter before the phone was switched off in haste. if you can't lie to your wife, who then?

gave la Belge some lavender and headed out. i wanted to watch the mind under pain / stress / long etapas trying to reach my 25th of October goal... well, do it - just do it. carry on with intention embraced.

re-experiencing the Calle de Christo slum-ugly entry into Viana, and thinking it could use a sewer water to wine miracle... but the albergue is not there. situated literally on the edge of town it shares the sheer prow-like cliff park, overlooking plains below, with a ruined roofless and wall-crumbled Cathedral... a skeletal shadow-cast Caligari Expressionist proscenium for summer concerts or besotted latenight oration.

the only familiar faces in the albergue are the Austrian couple i saw back at the Lorca café, where she had her two hands wrapped around a heavy frothy beer for a 10H breakfast - prost!

short September days... cold September mornings... "N'ayez

pas peur. C'est moi." ...and body within the body meditations churning.

V

    when the suddenly sky
        remembered me i
  stopped to pick one wild lavender scape,
      pungent and faded grey ~
wind wicks sweat away
    writing sacred salt-white runes upon my
        plains and blue mountain
            gazing brow

VI

shrub-tossing a dark morning
    apple core ~
hot with the jacket on,
    too cold with it off ~
drinking dovetailed-palm-bowl wine from th' Irache fountain
    blows brightening breath upon
        dawn's ember-cloud lit trail

VII

tilled red earthen breast
      exposed to light blue sky,
    late October asparagus crop's
        fine feathery green fronds whiffle down a
           foggy valley plain,
the 10,000 crimson rosehip watchful eyes

      *

    vine-robbed black grapes
        sourly dropped upon a sun-bleached
            trail, which in odd alchemy reddens where muddy...
    goat-shit beans, centipedes,
        slugs heading for
            damp ditch hollows ~
th' innumerable passings in a day,
    walking alone in wonder

VIII

e'er unfolding plains' patchwork
    rusts and greys in
    rumpled quilt undulations ~
        one white-thread trail
            meanders to its vanish
    in a horizon mountain fold

Viana - Nájera

woke to the plashing of hard rain in streetside rain-rapids... woke to the sound of wind-blown sodden leathery leaves.

up at 5:30H and downstairs among the mudroom's boots, bikes, and staffs... packing stuff-sacks with damp clothes.

from behind the pastelería counter i got a winsome smile but a poor palmera. dark descent winding out of Viana among high-walled backyard gardens and ramshackle wisteria-braced tool, tackle and kindling sheds... and then out into the mews. a darkness-obscured toss of a crappy palmera on someone's compost heap.

fierce winds raging through the fields.

she invited me in... that ineffably gentle old woman whose fig tree shaded home is a physical and spiritual downy cradle on the Way. the slick oilclothed front-room table spread out with toasts, jam, butter, snacks... the heartening scent of burned coffee. we chatted and i bought a scallop shell from her. her mother greeted peregrinos for over twenty years here, and she has been doing so for four, ever since the elder's death. she's either a witch or a technically advanced soul with motion sensors as she was waiting wrinkled elbows on the half-door when i came down the hill. and while visiting she hefted herself and waddled to the door just seconds before two cyclists came rolling by - she offering... "Sello? Sello?" there must be something in Christian Camino Mythology still threaded in the Spanish soul... something about a part of one's intentions going along with the pilgrim to the Saint's tomb, so determined are the many who want to stamp our Credenciales. with a few exceptions i prefer the sello to reflect where i've slept. the sello from this physical and spiritual downy cradle on the Way is one of those exceptions.

thinking i could avoid the coming storm front, i pressed steps into Logroño... by the cypress-lined park, by locked cemetery gates, over the river... shell emblems mortared into the cobbled street, past the facade of the Church of Santiago. there are many iconic stances and iconic actions of many saints - Joan of Arc in battle gear, St. Francis holding a dove, St. Anthony holding the Christ Child. all depictions of Santiago Matamoros, i.e. St. James the Moor-Slayer - disgust me. the representation of the slaughter of any group, for the advancement of Christianity, is a pathetic object of ornamentation and they should be removed from all churches. the prevalent opinion argues that this is 'art' and part of the Treasury of the Holy Catholic and Apostolic Church... however i rebut, fuck that. screw them to a museum wall. decor should not be the lodestar for a place of worship.

in a café for a Cola Cao... bartender blowing his nose laughing, 'That's what you get eating off the kids' plates!'

proceeded out through the rolling green municipal park with young spindle-trunked trees, to the reservoir parks and paths beyond. stopped at Marcelino's picnic table for a purple fig, and homemade membrillo on bread... an affable man with a harmonious mindset. he's out here every day giving coffee-thermos support to the pilgrims and handing out yellow-arrow-painted acorns and stones with the pilgrimage year writ in black on the back. wants nothing. says people think he's crazy, but then again - there are worse things than thoughts.

like the glen of balanced stone cairns in Aragonia... here's another point of concentrated peace and calm. below the sky-eclipsing statue of a bull's silhouette, between the sawmill and the highway, peregrinos have woven twig crosses by the hundreds into the mesh hurricane fence.

Navarrete in the distance... the scent of exotic spice.

i felt strong and strode rhythmically. started by-passing more people who left from albergues this side of Logroño - faces changing rapidly for my two 40K days. 40K days don't lend themselves to a Camino family forming, and without a family the repetitive water torture trickle of 'hi, how are you, where you from, where and when did you begin' leaks in. black mold spreading in the attic... a storm-uprooted tree's empty blooms.

stepping into the church in Navarrete... the retablo is cocooned behind dense latticework scaffolding. one aproned artisan on her back cleaning, painting, re-gilt-leafing the intricacies of seraph, saint, and holy birth to holy murder scenes. what section was completed and lit was glimmeringly brilliant. it will be an amazement when finished.

after a height of land... red earth, green vines, mammoth clouds rich with ocean-energy migrating, fronting over the northern Asturias mountain range.

day-long and prodigious 'repercussions' from these apples and the raw onion in the leftover breakfast bocadillo... wink. i'm a 'wind' mill!

a whole group of hospitaleros manning the albergue desk in Nájera today - pushing the Rioja wine, offering melon and grapes when i sat down for sello and payment. Sgt. James Friday thinking... just the bed, man. just the bed. cold back-lashing shower water. barely got wet. soaped up junk, cleft and cranny and called me laved.

laid sleeping bag out on the mattress and punctiliously organized my stuff-sacks there-on in like a bloated row of polychrome ticks across a dog's back. postage stamp kitchen and the burners are already full... in no mood to be jostled so i made another finger-lickin' guaca-dillo on the more spacious table. the Mexican woman next to me, after spilling dry rice all over table and floor, commented on my well-assembled sandwich... how we eat first with our eyes. apparently many eyes ate my sandwich first, then observed its bestial consumption. as stories were told it mythically grew like the weight of the one that got away.

again, not much time to engage with the twisting streets, sites, or river between arrival, ablutions, writing, eating, and settling in. Castilblanco de los Arroyos regrets resurfacing.

IX

staff swinging
    striding strong,
burping up last night's left over for breakfast
    tomato, avocado, onion bocadillo ~

    *

hurricane crash tide winds
    whip dark morning tree limbs,
        rake grapevines leaf-bare,
    and high power-lines wail with windwood reed-throated
        Mongolian dual-note ululations...

    *

oncoming flare-winged storm front that's
   got no bones about blackening
      Orion or the light blue
         in eastern skies ~

           *

WHAT is it in the Lear-ian
   tempest lasht plains
      makes me bellow baritone arias
'til balls bang high Holy Day
      Cathedral bell hammers...
         galaxial spirals swim the mind
            round vertiginous glowing
               eyes
               going black.

           *

   waking in birdsong sunlight ~
      the body in the body unbinds

X

over ferrous-rose earthen rows
   grapevine leaves autumnally turn
      blood burgundy with gilded veins ~
   swollen purple udder-fruit-clusters hang
      giving cheek, breast, and brow
         to bead the coming silver rain ~
and among fragrant rosemary leaves
   lite purple fairy-thimble blooms
      brighten my eye...
         i snap a twig for tomorrow's stew

Nájera - Santo Domingo de la Calzada

for fault of the third whiskey and an obsessive late-night internet search for the several lines of 'St. Francis and the Sow' i couldn't remember... for that, i forgot my leather change-pouch by the coin-op computer at the albergue. the couple Euros contained within... no loss. but i liked that Sainte Germaine medallion from Pibrac, and the heavy Arabic coin i picked up two years ago from a like a broke-open-trove strewn blanket in the Burgos flea market.

last night at the bar owned by a Spanish / Thai woman with an adorable chubby-cheeked daughter, who slowly warmed to me, shyly approaching to play toss with her unwieldy pink pig ball... last night at the bar a German and his wife came over with greetings, paused, smiling... i think waiting for me to invite them to sit down. she mumbled something Teutonic and he said "We won't disturb you." the actual present energy is to be away from the crowd. noting that 'body in the body' contemplations don't involve others... a fragmented faith opaques the heart. St. Augustine's, "Fill yourself of what you are empty and empty yourself of what you are full," should be the object of rumination for a spell.

indignant about the sign, 'no lights before 6:30H.' got up at 5:30H and lugged my whole kaboodle quietly into a back boot-room and layered ascendingly 'heavy to light' in the backpack.

left in the pitch dark... up through the pines and red rock cliffs, (as memory holds them in now's darkness), and out through sweeping grapevine plains. after Azofra... golden haybale towers yang the infinite blue sky.

once lush and spicily scented... now dead, dried, and leafless i broke through the hops field's 20 foot high pole-rows to the sounds of bells - sheep bells ringing. a herd and the herd's smiling Navarra-blue overalled shepherd making their way from grazing one stubbled field to graze another stubbled field. slow movement manifested beneath the dark water-heavy clouds blowing cold down from the north. these cloud talons reach deeper inlandly late afternoon and night, but the midday's sunbeams seem to prod them at bay away.

dusty roses, greys, fresh cut green stubble, golden hay rolling away before the descent into Santo Domingo... and i passed the restaurant where i feasted so well two years ago. looking forward to 20H when the comedor opens!

stepped into the municipal albergue after ablutions... said i forgot my change purse last night and it was right there sitting on the desk. she said a cyclist dropped it off this morning. the cyclist is long gone. no one to thank so i left thicker tips here and there that his kind energy may be echoed.

the Cathedral was entertaining two firecracker camera-flashing bus tours... not really a place of refuge and meditation at all. the cloister was closed off and shuttered into a hallway museum. and i had to pay to get in to see a pair of medieval myth chickens behind glass. shit like this just feeds my petulance. the Christ would have kicked their till-table over.

that guy has been on my mind... we never hear much about what i think is one of the greatest things the historic Jesus did in his life as a teacher - that of taking 'The Lord God Almighty,' 'The Majesty,' 'The Most High,' and all the other Old Testamental deific encryptions... and replacing them with 'Abba,' which means 'Papa,' which means - whatever our concept is of the Divine - that relationship is, in its nature, intimate and personal from the very start...

having a whiskey getting ready for my meal at Los Caballeros... dawdling the nib...

harvest time in the vineyards... itinerant gypsy help, caravan convoys, tractors pulling wagons the bandolier strapped hand buckets are emptied into.

and it is getting cold - getting worried. should have kept that thermal shirt i mailed back home from Salamanca.

some in France, but especially here in Spain i've come to love the 'cast iron plant.' the dark-green leafed Aspidistra decorating low-lit church alcoves and chapels whose opaque panes hardly illuminate the painted stone walls within. for ages of now bone-dust priests inviting spirit to the feast in fervent reverence or droned fatigue... the Aspidistra's rhyzomed leaves have softened pupil-wide eyes through time.

woman who runs the hostal i'm staying at said Los Caballeros did away with their bar and made the business solely restaurant...

...and nothing has changed but for the better to my mind. a 1999 Viña Ardanza before me... the bouquet of straw-bound green tobacco leaves drying in oaken attics...a jamón Ibérico plate with my own little bottle of green drizzle-dancing olive oil...

seared morcilla - blood sausage stuffed with rice, a hint of pepper spice, and surrounded by sautéed red pepper filets. nose, tongue, mind imaginations. before i die fly me here and feed me.

now this dish of grilled bacalao topped with toasted almonds over a leek purée and deep-fried spinach leaves!

torta del abuelito arrives - dear grandfather's tart? ...some sort of thin custard and crushed almond pie drizzled with honey and a caramel sauce.

XI

between October
    low southern sun arcs and northern
ocean cold winds... storm-dark clouds blow.
       the front's fragments cast
   my shadow into all
      crisp, blur, and fade-to-vanish shades ~
cold fingers and dripping nose
       falsely define my being...
     distant rain veils sweep
         the dusty-rose tilled field a darker carmine

XII

      haybale towers
   watch a rippling field-side stream
 channel last night's rain...
the pervasive silence.
    invisible ground wrens chortle through shorn-to-stubble fields,
      the silver light blue sky ~
in albergue society i am ruptured, swept
   and threshold dust wind-whisked away

XIII

walked out into diamond star facet shine spilt upon
     black velvet night,
  heart and belly tight with Tituba tales...
       'blood claw cooling-corpse-a-ditch' mind

    *

    this tipping earth dips the sky-fringe
       into pale blue pooling time,
           vast grapeleaf plains twitch out
              shudders knowing frost
                 bodes death and snow,
    the bird whistles red-cliff songs
and my tramping jostled eyes,
        more foul than fair,
           watch
        dim opal-glow trail rocks
            leap lustrous from close dark veils

      *

amber tractor beacon flashes
    shuttlecock tight switchback furrows
        across an invisible hillside.
silent night   holy dawn
   ripping fruit-fed breakfast
      wind
   in majesty's morn...
eucharistic, my flesh
    melts upon
       the palate ground

Santo Domingo de la Calzada - Belorado

giggled all the way home from that fine meal. she gave me a shot of orujo just to set me up right.

from precise albergue organizational ways i tend to explode stuff-sacks in a hostal room and it took some time to reassemble the backpack. left before 7H... a similar morning. a mild chill that got colder as day broke. accidentally took the Variante and added 4K to the etapa, but it was well away from the Nationale. and from my roundabout view, while the sun was in those low-angled degrees between horizon and cloudbank... long amber rays strike a colossal earthen breast pubescently bosoming up from the flat plains, complete with rocky outcropped nipple balefire-glowing beneath dark clouds.

turning into Grañón, a ruined house... two dogs through a wrecked upstairs window casement yowling savagery! stomping paws and torquing bodies to rip such barghest snarls from out their tortured souls - a riot! and my laughter made them roar more primal howls. i felt like Damien at the zoo. went down to the plaza for a coffee, and in front of the café there's a familiar scene - peregrinos' backpack, staff, water-bottle, boot, and bicycle paraphernalia strewn...

Castildelgado. bumped into two Italianos. bought a chocolate croissant from a flour-and-ash dusted man in a part-bakery / part-home, chimney billowing black woodsmoke.

in Viloria de Rioja i spied a new albergue run by Brazilians. their flag's constellated blue sphere on a yellow rhombus in a field of green, snapping in the breeze. went in to say "Bom dia!" and who is seated there beneath a five foot tall portrait of ole smiling Paulo Coelho but the Brazilian hospitalero who was working at the Calzadilla de la Cueza albergue two years ago, the day i slogged through cold driving rain! the hospitalero who didn't want to let me in! i wasn't aware, then, of the general 14H entry time to the albergues and all he said was "Everyone ees at thee barh." said i'd rather shower and change into drys before going anywhere and he moved aside laughingly, permitting me to pass like Oedipus on the query-stiled bridge out of Thebes. i remember he spent a lot of time mopping up the floor behind dripping wet peregrinos... the pack of unspayed bitches. that's the place i first saw people stuff wet boots with newspapers to wick away the wet.

at some point today the northern cloud-front got its umbilical cut and dark cloud herds ranged south polishing the horizon a shiny light blue, which deepened overhead suggesting the universal night beyond... this pinprick of a sphere... walking this pinprick of a sphere.

from a paneless window hang strung red peppers in vermillion clusters drying against dusty golden stone... the windowsill thick with flowerpots... calico cats haunt a sunny half-door.

this new Belorado albergue has a soothing fountained back-garden... there, a seal club of peregrinos bask, stitching clothes and feet. new beds, loud Spaniards, the Americans from Cincinnati and Tennessee are here, Californian cyclists are on the way, the rice-rain Mexicanas who loved my sub, the Québecois at the restaurant last night who irked me when they got flustered when the waitress didn't understand their English... you're in their country, and you're using slang! attractive and amiable light black German women - one loves cookies, one loves chocolate. only two showers per floor.

hospitalero is cooking up a vat of garlic soup with minced chorizo... i like how that compliments the paprika theme.

Ravi Shankar's daughter's CD playing endlessly at the albergue. if she can't figure out why she can't, she should try that African yohimbe 'bean' cream. being a word-hound i wondered on the etymology of that particular noun-verb. did an internet search and found what may be its first written / recorded usage, in the orgasmic sense, in a 1650 poem called 'Walking in a Meadowe Greene' ...about a chap who finished too quickly:

They lay soe close together, they made me much to wonder;
I knew not which was wether, until I saw her under.
Then off he came, and blusht for shame soe soon that he had endit;
Yet still she lies, and to him cryes, "one more and none can mend it."

after eating, a whiskey... a paseo through this village's cobbled together walls and streets... dwelling upon today's trail, upon the flora and fauna - the same or the spawn of those i've met before and meet now in mutual recognition. it is emotive... transcendent... a clearing in the Walden Woods... the Over-soul a-shine in a forest pool.

XIV

Santo Domingo de la Calzada's
    disembodied Cathedral spire
        bonfire-flame flickers
    down with walked-away distance and steeping dawn ~
as far as the eye can see, fields respire silence.
    blessings be upon those four steps
        stepping me from
    acrid goat-shit-mulched cropland effluvium
        to shorn wheat's sweet
            fermentation haybale piles, four blessèd steps...
tree leaves clinking with the chill
    in October morning breezes

Belorado - Agés

cracking eye open to latenight noise i spied one of the cocoa German women completely dressed, backpacked, and taking off at just after midnight. found out later she didn't have a watch and her internal clock thought it to be about 5H. she ended up coming back in and sleeping on the kitchen floor because, not only was my bunkmate above snoring, but talking loudly in his sleep! after much ribbing and laughter later in the day he said he's always done that... used to drive his mother nuts.

got up at 5:30H. moved my stuff away from sleepers into the kitchen light, woke her up, heated me orts of stew and ate some fruit. offered her a handful of tea bags and walked out of Belorado... a dark and mild morning going cold in the post-dawn.

passing by a picnic area outside Tosantos - dog barks - two sleepingbagged silhouettes sit up, "Buen Camino!" from the shadows... scrawny tattooed German pilgerin on the road. they used the albergue shower last night, then carried on, preferring to sleep wrapped in down and night.

in Villambista's La Taberna, like a genie in a jar, Inake fulfills café con leche and hot chocolate wishes! the black-bearded Basque bartender - welcomingly baritone and muy amable... wanting to see with precision where we're all from in his greasy kitchen-shelved Atlas tome. that Aussie woman was a bit curt with him. she thought he was 'cheeky.' the two Italianos showed up shouting greetings through the door with New Year's Eve's festivity! Mexican Daphne and her sister... the cocoa Germans wearing backpacks as large as themselves... we all hung out for a while... enjoyed the easy tidalness of the day... walking, café / bar stopping, peregrinos amassing, walking, stopping, congregating, carrying on... a pleasant pulse and flow.

Villafranca Montes de Oca. remembered the truck-stop feel to the place, and a steep climb up to the long row-planted pine forest to San Juan de Ortega. (craving taco dip).

stopped in Agés. absolutely nothing here years before but mellow meditation memories in Iglesia Santa Eulalia de Mérida... now, two brand-new albergues! stayed in the private but will eat in the municipal. sweet chubby alberguista at the expresso machine reminds me of Digna, an old friend from El Salvador who cooked for many years at the Café Pamplona. talked to her about Josefina and Spanish food. if the head cook permits she might make me a tortilla de patatas stuffed with morcilla and topped with a béchamel. right on! and Dyn-o-mite! Jimmy the Walker's gonna eat tonight!

got to buy gloves and a thermal in Burgos. this morning the cold made pain.

XV

gossamer V-cloud wings and the star-swan
    soar dark skies toward
        the amber bonfire blaze of
            morning moonset ~
through filigreed starlight lace
        a diamond-chip-flash meteor's graze
      ignites one mortal wish
              the ever laughing bright toothed Tao
            snips

XVI

rising gold sun hinges the ragged
    mountain horizon,
        cold cold wind blows

XVII

snacking on banana,
    green apple, couple fists full
        o' nuts
    makes morning
        flatus mighty

XVIII
   from how
      how many days hiking through
          shorn-crop plains...
now upon the Villafranca Montes de Oca mountain heights
    breathing down deep core pine,
      sternum oak,
        purple heather heart,
   broom in the cōleus' thick nest,
an easy boxwood white-toothed smile ~
    wind does more than rattle copse leaves here...
      forested mountainside gales
        crescendo anthems to skies
          cobalt-blued by
      th' universal night just beyond...
    and her warm breath velvet upon my peregrine ear

Agés - Tardajos

'Digna' made me that tortilla stuffed with morcilla and topped with a béchamel last night... a hundred kinds of delicious. sat with a Spanish crew who invited me into the fold. i starvingly wolfed down a bowl of carbonara, wine, some tortilla, ate half of their way-way-underdone albondigas, (meatballs). screw verotoxigenic E. coli. i was famished.

a serious granite-eroding rain pounding outside.

woke early. mashed an already half-mashed backpack banana with the plum jam they set out - that, with some olive oil and salt spooned over toasted bread - yeah. and a cup of thermos-warm coffee brewed the night before. i've paid a bundle for a restaurant meal and been less satisfied.

a warm and mystic fog-balmed morning, dark late for the overcast aube. soft morning steps through Atapuerca... panadería woodsmoke and fresh bread scent. at the top of a steep climb stretches a predominating cross - after the cross, a broad hilltop heath's spiral of gathered small stones. traced the broad hilltop heath's spiral of gathered small stones slowly with my eyes and added three more to the tail-end of the spiral with the sense of adding something to the path for others.

rambling through fog-gauzed hillscapes down to Villalval, interlacing hill slopes in the brume slowly reveal and whitely fade. felt the spiral turning softly on the center brow, swirling the warm dale-wide breeze into my spirit - swirling, massaging, easing, energizing... relaxing eyes, temples, brow, mind. the plantar planting peace.

the Riopico trilogy of hamlets... had a Cola Cao in the first tumbledown bar looking like a beachbum's hovel piled with collected flotsam. so glad i didn't take any of the Variantes suggested by the Spaniards in order to avoid the industrial entry into Burgos. i would have missed the vortex hill. and it really wasn't that bad... only the first section was industrial. the next - ugly residential apartment sprawls but with all variety of shops on the street level for distractive peering. saw the hospitalière from Lescar getting on a bus. thanked her for the washing machine and the butter... cinnamon black tea and toasted chestnut risotto memories.

Burgos has a monumental city center but despite the slight urge to stay i carried on. another Camino feeling strengthened by the hilltop spiral's magic... that of not seeking to 'visit' but of dwelling in Apparition. and with the idea of continuing 10K on to Rabé de las Calzadas, which according to the guide had an albergue with a kitchen, i bought lots of vegetables from a handshakes and smiles grocer before making my way out through suburbs, through poplar plantations... thinking of my coming meal.

Kibosh! both albergues were closed due to a plague of bedbugs! turned around to face an apogee to perigee black avalanching storm front! and made my way way back to Tardajos, stopping a French couple from continuing on to Rabé for the 'punaise' infestation.

shrivelingly cold shower at the albergue. hospitalero here knows Ana Maria, ('Digna'), who made me that tortilla last night. he attended her 'cocido' feast in Agés last weekend! ...a brothy aromatic boiled dinner of sorts with lots of garbanzos and chorizo.

the closed albergue signs were posted in four languages and the English translation for bed bug is 'thumbtack,' which kept me guessing for a moment. 'you're closing for that? get a dustpan!' then i read the sign in French. i hear the Italianos are here at the albergue and see the French couple i diverted, outside... all others bear new faces. i guess this'll be my familial wave for a while.

XIX

listening to hard night rain
      hit street-side flowing run-off streams,
           dreams turn to
torture   corpse   blood.
   waking gape-eyed and breathless in fear wondering
      where these foreign-room windows are in the blackness...
        guts, an overcooked noodle bowl ~
clicking wooden wrist beads for a moment makes me smile

      *

    dark-red wet morning earth steams,
      fumeroling
    field, copse 'n forest.
an otherworldly bird cries white ripples in the fog...
   treading gravelly ground
      sole-silent as i might...
not shook off enough and tucked away
   damp shorts spot
      cools glans in the brume

XX

cloud socked-in hilltop hike,
    a pebble-nipple-pile centered spiral,
        the Milky Way ancient eddy quivers and rasps
            alone upon the fringe-vanisht world -
from the nipple i trace eyes slowly over
    all these earth-bone bits
        pilgrims' hands held, considered
            and placed into cirrus grace.
clacked three stones down by the
    last colimaçon coccyx tip
        and slipped into the fog away,
            brow whirling, spiral breeze alive

Tardajos - Castrojeriz

one of those quick close-night-eye / open-morning-eye sleeps devoid of R.E.M. - barely restful. woke early with the Italianos... so funny. so loud! it is a physical impossibility for them to be quiet. i even heard them trying - five words of tight-throated whispering then BAM! volume up to level 11! the hospitalero had two black thermoses of coffee, one of milk, and a basket of bread waiting on the desk downstairs - simple and thoughtful. left him the carrots, zuchini and onion i never cooked... damned thumbtacks.

knowing the back-tracked road well i headed out, and into magical beauty... pure beauty! the stretch between Tardajos and Rabé de las Calzadas was a swirling enlacement of full-moonlit fog floes flowing in and out of form, the primordial potential a gypsy sees upon uncovering her crystal ball. an easy climb up through misty fields until the sun slowly shifted all to pale-blue and lighter. the fog, thick with cumulative eye-level distance, thinly above let a few stars pierce through. stars vanish and full moon fades revealing idiosyncratic isle outcroppings - these 'out of my plow's way!' stones for centuries thrown into quarry piles in which all manner of windblown and rodent hoarded seeds have taken root... strange isle outcroppings adrift upon the plain.

in the widespread nothingness a valley dipped - Hontanas in its embrace. wended down to the church plaza... peregrinos' strewn boots and backpacks, Italianos eating tortilla bocadillos, and others arriving. a woman sweeping the terrace... i congratulated her. "¿Por qué?" said last time i was here the entry to Hontanas was a dump, all scrap metal and trash. now it's clean except for one lone broke-down truck they seem to be mowing around. motorized parachuters soaring high above this quiet stone and Sunday village.

left Hontanas looking forward to sitting among the dove-cooed San Antón ruins again... but for unsafe and crumbling walls it is closed now. glad, at least, to photograph the Tau intersticed rose window - long bereft of colored glass. in memory's shadow i peeled a spiny chestnut souvenir to roll Baoding round the fingers.

walked into Castrojeriz and headed for the small private albergue - two years new... young bohemians running the place with dogs and guitars. in the rickety barnboard-cobbled dorm room i tried to make conversation with a bandage-headed man who did nothing but stare at me dumbly. for crying out loud you can say in your own language that you don't understand and we can go from there...

followed the long meandering main street down to this soothingly shadowed bar whose mellow fluted music... ah, say oasial. "oasial," they say...

not much going on but not looking for much. sat with beers, the Italianos, Nottingham Brit, the Aussie and a quiet German woman. Lukas from Poland came by looking to use the bar's internet for a spell. he was just passing through. another one who prefers to sleep outside.

supper's bocadillo was a joy. bought cheese and bread from the warm-hearted woman at the El Lagar Bar. and in the albergue's fifth floor crow's-nest of a kitchen... heated oil, rosemary, garlic and grated carrots on high in the microwave and then spooned that over the tomato, onion and cheese sandwich - luscious.

XXI

combing fingers through
    cool fog-wet hair,
full moon sings silent phosphorent rings
    across the sky,
        faint trail-side tree silhouette
            emerges into close precision
                walking out well before dawn...
      my flesh, the chariot...
          my eyes, reins...
mind drawn by full west settling
    moon across
        the broad fog-gentled
            Meseta plains -
invisible bird cries
    ripple elegant Mu hieroglyph wisps,
        invisible bird-flight wings lightly leave
            the Three Dharma Seals gyring in diaphanous air...
one gleaned from the fog
    drop drips off my
        feather-blessing brow
            and brow spirals deeply
with the lappably close
    blue velvet rolling
        cheshire cat's-eye marble moon

XXII

October light blue sky,
    white popcorn clouds course over
        the unbounded Meseta plains

       *

chill west wind,
    cropt crops gone,
when mind is still
    invisible ground wrens'
        woven song seems
the earth herself
    AH!
THE EARTH HERSELF
    chittering, chortling, shimmering,
        whistling
            timeless time along ~
a trail,
    a booted man blisters,
        a wild quince grows
            to perfume little Eliodora's linen drawer
            within the matrix of time

Castrojeriz - Frómista

after a few moments hanging with the hospitaleros, guitars and dogs - went to bed. the room filled up - loud Spanish peregrinos. one without segue tripped immediately from speech to snore and did not stop. when he did suddenly cease making sound in the pre-dawn i almost got up to check his pulse... almost. everyone's gotta go sometime and i figure if i'm staying i might as well get a few hours' rest.

lightning storm's strobe-flash 'n rumble lasted all night.

really wanted to lie late in bed but, remembering the past few beauteous mornings i hauled stuff-sacks into the reading room and repacked. in the bathroom a flustered Québecois angrily bemoaning the lack of a hook to hang his t-shirt from while he shaved. "It's an inexpensive thing! Why can't I have a hook?!" easy pal. chauffe pas ta pisse.

Bandage Head left first... i followed his solitary bootprints for a long while in the mud. at Fuente del Píojo, 10K out, i came across Lukas emerging tortoisely from his make-shift picnic table and tarp tent... said the storms were amazing!

final steep climb up to the highest expanse of these Meseta tablelands... an immense and flat tract of geography reaching out 200K. the two Italianos were there atop when i pantingly arrived... hands on hips like guards saying stentoriously, "Yoo marcha fuerte!"

at the Boadilla del Camino lee-shaded outskirts a mongrel mutt watched me eat dried pears and nuts, then slunk his low-cast eyes out to the poplar-lined canals... poplars, torrential rushing locks lifting and lowering water across the plains. Frómista! Pension Marisa - a room, ablutions, a nap... clothes and boots drying in the rooftop SUN! dry at last!! dry at last!! thank God almighty, dry clothes at last!

the American cycling family from Puente la Reina is here, lounging in the plane trees' limb-woven shade, switchblade slicing dried sausages and cheese. mop-head 'Nick' told me about a book called <u>Backyard Ballistics</u> which i can't wait to buy for all the boys i know! yeah, the chandelier is shattered... but he built the trebuchet that flung the stone!

sitting on the park-bench beside me a chubby German expressed her scowly jowled contempt for American 'this' and American 'that' assuming i stood for 'this-and-that' by nature of my birth without asking me my opinion. as she slowly pitched away i mugged at her like a bratty 4-year-old and was busted by a toothless granny cracking up from an omniscient upper window.

XXIII

last night's paparazzi lightning
    strobed phantasmic shadows on make-shift and tilting
        albergue walls. beneath last night's albergue window
            one hell-dog yowled at distant thunder...
    through partridge-wing-banded clouds
        this dark morning's pearl moon
            trails tilling beam tines through shorn crop-stalk
            stubble,
        winks from muddy puddles,
and in Yahweh finger ways
    kindles mire into one westward walking magi
        strolling breath upon these moon-bright plains...
            brow spirals,
                tantien belly churns

XXIV

dew-lustrous crimson
    rosehips bead
        royal wren throne-throat decrees
touching all what is lovely between
    the pale setting
        moon and dawn's
            golden sunrise,
touching with eyes all that
    her song does with sound

XXV

cloud shoal shadows skim
    the tan wave-land plains,
        one levee-mounded canal
          flows highly through it all...
through it all the whispering reed-fringed oasis serpentines.
beyond meticulously aligned October-golden poplar tree plantations,
    locks, overflowing with the sturm und drang surging onslaught
      of
        last night's rain...
church bells behind fade
    church bells ahead bright,
        waving constant flies from
          my face away,
    inviting there be peace behind my eyes

Frómista - Calzadilla de la Cueza

hung out in yesterday's airy upper room. made a snake-jaw snapping thick sub, drank some wine - ate, sash-to-spine nestled in the window casement overlooking mottled clay tile rooftops and the clattering backside of a small restaurant down below... reading Pagnol under formless skies, steeped in sunlight and his rich vocabulaire...

finished off the sub-butt for breakfast and left before 7H. the two Italianos bellowing HELLOs and BUEN CAMINOs in the silent morning. pressed darkly on. Población de Campos! in the polygonally streetlight pane-cast vacant road something bit me wicked hard and i whirled drunken Dervish circles with ambushed surprise - ! - wasp? spider? vicious type of fly? just saw something alien and black clinging to me and i whacked at it repeatedly before its six or eight legged release. a sharp itch-infested pain in the calf-tender below the back bend of my right knee.

saw Lukas the tent-Pole's make-shift bivouac draping another picnic table beneath the wisping cloud flames of early day.

a difficulty i'm trying not to exacerbate in repetition, but... 5K before Carrión de los Condes and 10K after - thought i was crazy. and when i realized i wasn't i imagined i would be soon! those horrific flies! swirling swarms of small black flies bouncing off eyes, nose, cheek, ears, mouth, ticking off hat brim - not biting, but the constant swarm and land, swarm and land, swarm and land... spent 15K constantly waving hand before my face, making me nauseous for the movement. and there's no Dramamine on this here plain.

trudged into Carrión and stopped in the pastelería where i sat in reminiscence enjoying a CCL and palmera. bought a bag of biscotti for to later charm the 'short' etapa post-Carrión de los Condes... a mere 16.8K which i believe is merely savage and ruthless, merely haunted, and merely the worst etapa of all my 2000 miles on the Camino. two years ago along this stretch - miserable driving cold horizontal rain. now, 10 more kilometers of flies unfold. FLIES! gratefully, thankfully, and finally Aeolus! a steady wind blew up from the south keeping them away, freeing my mind to 'focus' on inner foot pain traipsing these endlessly unbroken expanses.

Calzadilla de la Cueza albergue... three or four French speakers, one Brazilian, two German women but with oddly sculpted accents. made my ablutions quietly and came here to the bar... to the same table, chair and corner i sat in two years ago when the place was packed with soggy peregrinos and i sipped three fortifying-the-damp-away CCL's and three whiskeys, then stretched out on my lower bunk tented with wet poncho and wet clothes... twitchily napping to pass the time until dinner. ate a tasty braised rabbit that night. wonder what tonight's menú will present. heading back for a nap now and a poem. Calzadilla is a ramshackle commune. so rundown. even in Easter sunshine it would be depressing.

XXVI

  kamikaze, dumb or deific flies dive-bomb me
     bouncing bulging billi-facet eyes
        off cheek, brow, ear, nose
           eyeglass lenses
             WHY?
    i don't get it!
under the blue dome of heaven,
    under white billowing cumulonimbus towers' rise,
      under fit to burst black cloud bellies,
        on the limitless Meseta plains
    an insignificant man wondering why?
        i
do not hate you but would bear
    the songless silence while bird-dom
        hunted cracked carapace chewed consumed digested
      and shat you all out
          into
      the utterest extinction

XXVII

   in memory's song
      this sky long bird-of-paradise
         cloud form
       elegantly rose, slowly shifting, turning
          amber flared flame
           tendrils
from one western grey-stormed horizon...
      the last diaphanous eastest-reaching 'petal' tip
        flickers with dawn,
          unfurls and
   sky-arc flings a
full white marble moon...
      in writing's pause conditions unravel back into Beloved
         numena,
       heaven's flower vanishes
     save the petal-tossed pearl on velvet blue,
      and the scent of
        wild fennel rot
         stays too...
more lingeringly than vision and
    this spirit spattered page

XXVIII

my windshield-wiper-arm slowly swipes
     away demon legion sand grain infinite swarms,
       ineffectively.
   sight-speckling black flies
tracking eyeglass lenses, kamikaze crashing
   ear-wells, eye ducts, brow, cheeks,
      centepeding through beard whiskers, hocking
        black-wing-pitted spit
         splats in the withered
           trailside fennel shrubs...

feeling ever a breath away from
   the Meseta plains'
      plenary pandemoniac madness,
   humming peace-ease of mind Metta phrases
      with each bronze-armed
         swipe ~
may what today's burden brings
   on the morrow
      be bright

Calzadilla de la Cueza - Sahagún

letting routine habituals go - didn't pre-pack. no intention of getting up or out early... enough already with the goddamned morning moon. got trapped with other crap. German woman last night turned one bank of lights off and, mistakenly, another one on... then stomped around the dorm loudly gesticulate and Germanizing. she ended up singling me out for her tirade. i gave her a bandage-headed mute stare-glare, got up and flipped the switch to darkness again thinking, 'Jesus Christ woman this is a light switch not rocket science. What are you going to do when a real problem arises?' which having not said i repeated countless times in sleeplessness' silence. o mind!

the Brazilian, one bunk over, was first out in the morning. the noise he made passive-aggressively pleased me hoping he woke that mustard-pot Frau from her snoring.

examined the bite this morning... i see two long punctures so i'm going with the fanged-spider theory. surprised there's no welt, but there's a deep-in-the-meat blend of strong itch and sharp pain. venom and flesh. another 'lug your kit into the next room to pack quietly' practitioner joins me on the bathroom floor, cutting medical tape strips and binding her feet Chinese princess style.

leaving Calzadilla de la Cueza, mild overcast skies soon bruised and began to rain. thinking how i entered Calzadilla two years ago is hauntingly how i leave it now, but that sourness evolved into appreciation reflecting on the wind and rain keeping the flies away.

never too far from the carretera today.

shaking my head at these tiny communes i can walk through in two minutes, with crazy long names... Terradillos de los Templarios, where in 2004 i met a woman whose accent i could not place. in that frigid horizontal rain storm her entire journey's journal got drenched to an inky, pulpy mass. as a beneficent Dickensian apparition i think of her when i unwrap my Credential for daily albergue stamping, my journal for writing... both now sheathed in strong blue plastic sacs from the Gibert Joseph booksellers in France.

ducked a low lintel into the bar in San Nicolás del Camino - two young French guys, two older French women, a quiet German. one Française went multi-lingually on and on about what the erstwhile tool hanging on the wall was... the wooden runners with stone inserts inset in the grooves used to break up wheat from chaff. when she made her way to me, asking if i understoo-..."Thank you, yes. In all three languages. I got it." she stuck a feather and a fern frond in her hair, they all sang some French Camino promenading song, took photos of über-wide smiles and left in the image of a cartoon brawl... a rolling dust-cloud popping out and pulling in fist, leg, arm, head, hat, fern frond and 'shift numbered' curses... &#@$! they were replaced by a Spanish couple coming in i hold in high regard. these two have done the Camino Francés, what, six times? by now they don't even bring a camera and nary a pen... open only to the Way, be it bumpy or smooth. left a folded paper peace crane for the bartendress.

thinking i'd pass through Sahagún to Bercianos, 10K beyond, not wanting to wait until 16:30H for the albergue here to open...

standing in vacillation on the corner of Sahagún's compact Plaza Mayor watching a cloud morph, a woman asked me what i was looking for - then without waiting for a response she gave me directions to the Hostal Escarcha i saw advertised back at the low-linteled bar in San Nicolás. i'll take that as a sign. to the first bell i rang - nothing. to the second - older woman carrying an iron and a slip came down... sweet and generous. said as her son is away on vacation the restaurant is closed, so there's no demi-pension, but i can have a room. and she offered me the restaurant's kitchen to prep my fare.

undressing in the bathroom, dumping pebbles from my boot... a dead fly falls out. i won't take that as a sign.

heading in earlier, shining skies surrounded an immense black-cloud isle hovering over Sahagún and the sporadic rainfall scattered rainbows. tripping over Moses' sandals i was in awe among ROYGBIV flamed trees.

the storm front is gone now... a penetrant chill is left behind.

woman at the Hostal told me tomorrow is El Pilar... what? El Virgen del Pilar. another National Holiday where everything will be closed up tight. gotta buy supplies for tomorrow night, then, and haul 'em all day long. apparently while St. James was preaching in Iberia, things weren't going so well and he settled into prayer to ask for help. Mary heard him back in the old country, and since her Frequent Flyer stamp-book was well-filled, first class Hosts of angels puddle-jumped her over the Mediterranean, she appeared before James, and handed him a carved wooden statue of herself upon a jasper pillar. nice gift! here's a wood and stone sculpture of me to lug around. clearly she never backpacked without a mule.

going down to the restaurant's kitchen to cook over roaring foot-wide blue gas burner flames.

XXIX

cold wet fingers numb
    around the walking-stick, trudging
  like a bent against the storm beggar lurching forward,
      seeing naught but the
    stoney trail... naught but the stoney trail...
        long after gale-driven
    rain had stopped, seeing naught but the stoney trail
      and lost in lottery ¿y si toca? obfuscations -
  stopping,
watching
the autumnal poplar plantations' overarching canopies
      toss gold-leaf sprays windward away
    to panache black cloud-front mountains
        coming fast...
  smiling at the here and now absence of flies

XXX

pale golden light
  pools and plays upon
    weedy green grown post-harvest
      field furrows -
one solitary wind-bared-of-leaf hilltop tree Atlases
    the black boulder cloud
      avalanching sky

Sahagún - Mansilla de las Mulas

ahhh... that back-embracing mattress!

i don't recall much from the day. not much to recall. decided to take the Camino's left branch and followed the long westward heading bee-line of yellow-rusted-brown-and-green leafed young sycamore trees... how gorgeous will this shaded lane of lanes be in thirty years! snakes escaping my steps rustle hay... the spider bite tickle-itching in calf meat... achingly cold northwest wind blows from distant blue mountains... wooly sheep flock 'boulders' between vast sky and vast plains... moments of flies but not bad.

in Bercianos del Real Camino - between the bright white brick and yellow-trimmed trailside church and insouciant cats sunning on adobe window sills - nothing open. Thursday's El Pilar Sunday-silence. pressed on through, matter of fact i pressed on all day - 38K. only stopped for a few poetry notes, a few shrubby micturations, and the sudden fist-in-the-gut exhaustion on one shaded bench in Reliegos.

the light is incomparable, so low and golden...

got to the albergue in flat Mansilla - not full, but filling. cooked up a risotto right off. small kitchen. no desire to be sardine-packed, jostling pans and burners.

Nottingham Brit's the mine canary... the telltale harbinger that the Italianos are near.

XXXI
   my daybreak shadow sweeps long
      as to th' horizon reaching
         focal-line of sycamore tree leaves'
green, lime, spackled yellow, browns...
       seems
   each leaf has its own idea
      of the season's light ~
        my kind of tree.
dawn's baby blue o'er dawn's baby rose,
    didn't notice the stars fade
      but the moon still is a
        pearl reflecting pool.
   white visible breath,
      pissed grass steams,
and my once hundred-hues-of-russet chin slowly whitens to one...
      bare twigs
        bear buds...
you've stopped long enough Jimmy,
   and the trail draws on

XXXII

the molten-copper tilled plain
    glows
  in late October exposed
      to
    blue-shine white wisp skies.
faintly, far mountains'
    ragged crests seam
      Spanish earth
        to
      Spanish sky.
northwest chilly wind refreshes
  and this long-to-sight's-end
    sycamore line unfurls -
dried pear peanut water complex-carb breakfast
    ripping powerfully pure methane
      no lab could ass...
    the day blue
      silent moon

Mansilla de las Mulas - León

after eating early last night i had a hands-clasped-at-the-coccyx paseo and tiny vino tinto here and there...

woke at midnight to piss. wheelbarrow-fisted bunkbed beams and epileptically shook the snorer's bed beside mine into silence. slipped quietly out to the kitchen about 5:30H, bound feet, ate, dorm-room rustling begins.

walked the wide trail by the carretera - stars, awe-bright with the waning moon... barely adequate light to see. cold cold morning.

didn't realize it was Friday the 13th... it could have been disastrous had i been aware. rice-veg stew last night, wine, rice-veg stew for breakfast and a pot of tea don't make for easily retainable fecalities.

felt th' internal stir and rumble but like hell if i was going to bare ass 'n tender baggage in this frigidity and uncork in a black rockily rutted field. could have been tumbled-over disastrous had i been aware. but glory and praise be to you oh Puente Villarente's opened-so-early Pastry Shop and Bar with the Well-Vented John! but for plumbing the illusion persists that i am more than a naked ape.

major highway and industrial descent into León. there's going to be peregrino roadkill if they don't build a tunnel or a bridge. missed a turn in the suburbs and, scraping counter to every Y-chromosome within i asked for directions. psychology professor at the University with herpes simplex split-crust pus on her upper lip led me through a confusion of streets to a branch of the tourist office for a map - and joy-joy! an organ concert tomorrow night in the Cathedral!

in my tiny room, ablutions... clothes hanging by the window in no hurry at all to dry.

happy to be in León and know my way around. an ease in the marrow knowing no hiking tomorrow. will lighten my pack in the Correos, at last.

a familiar looking dirty German pilgrim approaches me with pop-eyed urgency saying while he was sleeping out under the stars vagabonds stole his backpack and could i please help him with some cash to get back home? looking at him squarely i replied, "The five Euros I gave you two years ago didn't seem to help. Maybe you should start walking towards Germany?" if you want... ask. don't take me for a friggin' stooge.

out for a pass-the-time paseo... sat with Lukas the tent-Pole, the Italianos and Nottingham Brit. "How do you put an elephant in the freezer?" "How do you put a giraffe in the freezer?" "Lion has a meeting with all the animals in the world before him but one...

what is it?" the litany of riddles i did quite well at. Nottingham is having a blast... "Nice life isn't it?" is his white-smiled refrain.

searching around for specific needs... near the post office where i mailed away so much weight i found a shop to buy a long-sleeve polypropylene undershirt! further down the road - a light fleece scarf and polyprop glove liners! further down the road - a ferctería to sharpen my knife! what a road! dropped it all off at the room then visited one of my favorite coffeeshops in the world - EKOLE! and am having a café Belmonte... in a tumbler pour 1/3 sweetened condensed milk, 1/3 brandy, and 1/3 expresso coffee, then dust with cinnamon! a famous toreador liked his joe this way and Belmonte was his name-o.

haven't visited the Cathedral or San Marco... preferring an afternoon dive-bar tortilla bocadillo and a dive-bar beer.

the search for 'gastronomic delight' ended here, on the corner of the elegantly arcaded Plaza Mayor. a cured embutido plate - prosciutto, cheeses, a cured loin - the deep red air-dried meat has the flavor of the wooden attic it was aged in. 2004 Tampesta - a Prieto Pecudo and Tempranillo blend from Valdevimbre... sure that this won't run through me like mountainside rainstorm mud. what a horror this morning could have been had i been aware. this Morcilla Leonesa plate is more of a chopped and stewed blood sausage for to spoon over croutons. as a kid i remember Pépère saying an old aunt on the farm made it similar to this, but topped it first with a white sauce then baked it. Mémère would fry it up in a pan with pork sausage, (because there wasn't enough fat in the boudin alone), then plate them with buttery mashed potatoes. and i'd wash it all down with a glass of cold whole milk that'd make him shiver. he thought the lot would solidify in my gut but at ten i wasn't into coffee. bacalao - lite breading... fried then stewed in an onion / bell pepper / tomato sauce - so pleasurable a meal.

Nottingham and Itali-Luka found the Nijmegen woman we met

back in Mansilla, crying on the Cathedral steps. when i saw her at the Correos she told me she had had a difficult day, but i didn't realize how difficult. cold morning, she hated the albergue, strayed aimlessly all around León with her backpack on... wished i had known. we could have had tea. being aware of how these vast and empty, open-to-the-elemental-sky plains stretch the soul to the snapping point is the best defense, but many first-time pilgrims aren't conscious of the phenomenon until they suddenly find themselves in mid-LSD panic-y freak-out. awareness of this potential allows what is stretched to relax instead of snap... and... a mirror please. internal storms, unsociable waves, and tirades explained.

thoughts of Miguel, a peregrino i met hiking with his dog after Mansilla de las Mulas two years ago... he showed me the local tradition of ordering a half beer or wine and getting a tapa gratis. after we hung out in one bar for a while, tale-ing, gnawing on pork ribs and beans - we left, and heading down the street... "Hey Mike," I says, "Where's your dog?" for conversation's perambulations we forgot the pooch tied to a gutter-pipe he ran back to and slathered with apologia, love, and hind-paw-thumping back-of-the-ear deep massages... then he vanished homeward for an uncle had died and he would return to finish the Camino later.

León

coffee by, then sat inside the Cathedral for a while breathing stillness. i think it's a Psalm: 'not in the rock shattering Wind, nor the Earthquake, nor Flame... but in a gentle Whisper the divine Presence came.' something along those lines. such elaborate vegetative stained glass - leaf, branch, vine, and grain patterns alternate with ecclesiastical imagery.

the market on the lower plaza was packing up... shucked-away bruised leaves, broken vegetables, rotten fruit and crushed damp-stain boxes exude a warm cabbagey scent... all waiting for the street sweepers' jet sprays and spinning wire brushes.

saw Uruguay Guillermo and Alex, (the sleep-talker from Belorado), across the square - familiar faces catching up. some South Americans, like the Galegos, add a whisper to their speech. the double 'l' is usually replaced by an 'x' in spelling, and in speech is pronounced like a soft 'sh.' lluvia - rain - is said [shuvia]. Guillermo - William - is said [Guishermo]. the Portuguese do their fair share of shooshing as well but their fricative is more centered around the 's' after a vowel. os dois carros - the two cars - is just one long leaking balloon!

twelve days to Santiago... remembering on the Vía de la Plata when i thought eleven days would be an incredible stretch. now after three weeks from Oloron - a drop... but not a drop. getting harder to carry on... the constant Meseta strain, darkening days, the paralleling seasonal and emotional contraction... season, man and mind contracting... once effusive summer's dwindling exhale. but there are mountains ahead - a positive change.

nonjudgmental attention... nonjudgmental attention... looking forward to feeling the weight of the pack with nonjudgmental attention.

XXXIII
walking out into pre-dawn
    night, the high
  half-moon pools shoulder-wide
      shadows round my ankles

*

lowly over the meadow,
> a clipt from the same black velvet bolt as night
>> invisible crow's wing
>>> strokes calligraphic serif eddies in formless groundfog,
> illuminating the sacred silence
>> between
>>> psalms
>>> ...
earth's first respiration
> nurtures morning nostriled lungs,
>> the morning eye-lit mind smiles

León - San Martin del Camino

the violin, cello and organ concert in the Cathedral was a pleasure. not a magnetic combination but the strings were rhapsodic. they set themselves up in the center choir amidst detailedly carved wooden bench-back crest rails and spindles, and ornately sculpt stonework, all back-lit. the center-nave ceiling arching hints of mythological heaven above. the contrast of the watery flow of bow-hummed strings around arabesque wood and stone was something to savor. leaving the concert... carved leafy Green Man faces emerge from an outer wall by the first Cathedral door. didn't see them in the light... vampyric stone.

happily-well-wrapped in new insulate clothes and leaving León through suburbs and warehouse rows... Sunday Industrial Parks oddly serene. bar with the memoried goldfish bowl among dusty liquor bottles was closed at this hour. stopped in la Virgen del Camino for a CCL and a corn muffin, and decided to take the way that followed the N120. working with internal peace instead of peace of place... listening to Dopplering car sounds come-exist-and-vanish. anyone can go zenny in a garden, but how are we on the asphalt?

stopped at the new albergue in San Martin del Camino after only

25K. early to stop, but then again a tired beginning. got a room for 7E, washed and hung clothes in the sharp boozy fermentation scent of autumn rotting quince... and for the absolute lack of any commerce here i'll be eating whatever menú the albergue offers tonight.

played in pooling timelessness with kittens and twigs.

San Martin del Camino - Astorga

the day was saved by three dogs... four actually.

took the highway-side trail again to work with 'harder surroundings' mind. probably would not have mattered much since i could have ranged through Glory and never known it for the residual cacophony that bitchy French woman last night left behind - full of ridiculous criticisms gleaned from TV watching. so high on her horse she must get tea-bagged nightly by Orion. how does it get under the skin? the multi-facets of disruption.

early this morning in mid-dream, the dog from yesterday came to me. the dog whose clawed paws i heard running on gravel... who then stopped to peer at me through the shrubs. magic's 'three times' running then stopping to watch, running then stopping to watch, running then stopping to watch - not a bark, not a yelp, not an anything. pure nonjudgmental attention. when i turned to look back at him the last time he just wagged tail and tilted head. he came to me in dream and i was bathed in sustained warm calm. two long-haired Spaniards hiking the trail, each with his own young pooch... first tawny flopfoot puppy leaving the bar smiled! the second slipper-sized white pup curled up on the barroom floor, wriggling to be greeted and pet. passing through San Juan a weathered gent stopped and wristed the curve of his cane... genially-eyed, 'where i'm from' pleasantries and shaking hands - the fourth old dog.

at the San Javier private albergue in Astorga... Javier's not here. hospitalero hasn't seen him in weeks. no one knows. mysterious vanishings. when i was here last it was his birthday and his wife was expecting... said he was going to go home and scare her to make her drop so he and daughter could share the nativity. the albergue is staffed now with all foreign hospitaleros and has an edge it didn't have before. courtyard, not as welcoming as it once was... the fountain is dry, geraniums are gone.

it's time to accept the feeling i do not want to be here. i do not want to stumble with foreign ears and tongues. excitement is gone or withered in a way i cannot restore... tired of churches and architecture, tired of religious art, tired of writing and the Camino, tired of regional food, and of feeling and numbing, tired of not understanding and the wariness of mind.

grey light. shuffling through syncopant rain. went to Merlin's Cave looking for a something or other to ground me. i know there's no sense in looking outward but i did anyway. one can make a case for the crutch. bought a smooth black and particularly cool-to-the-touch hematite.

listening inside to these ancient echoes i become aware of my eternity. cattari-ariya-saccani. disquietude, anxiety, unsteadiness and pain 'is.' 'is' has origination. 'is' ends. the Way to the cessation of 'is' is unfolding. acceptance first, then transformation. every rash and blister an open window to the Way.

in the back room of a pizzeria with fair wine... a cheese, tomato, roasted red pepper, olive, olive oil and anchovy salad... and a pizza with chorizo. the Spanish 'Who Wants to be a Millonario?' on the tube... some question about gerbils copulating 320 times an hour? come on!

more loud Spaniard's in the Cathedral pissed me off. i don't care anymore if it is their country. plug it! oi, every rash and blister...

XXXIV

watching sun swing slow
    shadows around trail stones,
        simply walking with a smile -
        the imagined invisibility
            that that
rubbish and weed wrack
    roadside banking cat
        thinks he has
            in stillness i think
i shatter staring
    into his haughty eyes... haughty eyes pretending not to meet
            mine.
        damn you!
    i'm trumped! by the
        smug bastard in ragged grass -
smile becomes laugh walking to, by, and past thee
    in eyes-to-sky stately poised unflinch.
        my body sinks into
            a cool oblique building-cast shade pool,
        the now only radiant
            October sun

Astorga - Foncebadón

woke early. left first. so dark. slight moon. slow climb. cloud and fog transforming the dark morning landscape up to Santa Catalina de Somoza. pulled into the bar... flashback. i know this is the same place i stopped in before, same Neander-brow working the coffee machine... but i have absolutely no memory of that stretch out of Astorga, the footbridge over the highway, or the slow climb - none at all.

'little wolf' growling the grundle.

El Ganso - Bar Texarkana. didn't stop in but the sombrero,

jalapeño light strings, cactus and cowboy kitsch festooned facade was familiar. i'd love to stop and support every place, drop a few Euros in each... absorb the scent of the den.

Rabanal del Camino - Mesón Gaspar. had a thick and savory tortilla bocadillo while people slowly caught up and came in... José / Midnight-Rambler Alex / Guishermo / Koala-Susan. knocked on the albergue door wanting to say thanks for the nurturing they gave me here two years ago when i was sick with the giardia. found out Susan belongs to the British Confraternity of St. James, which owns and runs that albergue, so i asked her to accept my thanks as no one answered the door.

the fog set in to soothe... aloe on a wound. we're high - 1400M. peaceful. gentleness in the air. the brume-sheened heather in dull purple bloom. trailside broom is thick. phasing fog forms from the valley below rushing up through scrub forests accompany me into ghostly Foncebadón... a steep, rill-eroded rubbly road winding through caved-in stone stonewalls, stables, broke-casement rooms and ruined roofs... a mountainside commune clubbed by elements and time. and amidst the debris - one playful Shepherd puppy with a roly-poly belly unsuccessfully tries to herd hissing geese.

the new Tibetan-decor albergue was welcoming. splashing ablutions in the sink thinking nothing will dry outside in this fog... hung what i laundered off the bed frame as all the troops were arriving in soundwaves downstairs.

went with Rambling Alex and Guishermo to a restaurant down the hill for snack and beer. AWESOME boar, game, stew, roast, ale, medieval restaurant with not a vegetable to be found beyond turnip and kale. Hrothgar's Hall! pelts soften the sooty stone walls... horns and antlers tangle their way into candelabra and sconce forms... all manner of hunted head-trophies hang from lacquered plaques on the walls... and like cave stalagmites on the tables, towering candle-wax drippage below a thatch ceiling!

José takes a digital shot of an abuelita bending down and throwing stones out of a gravel road... a ruined village like this needs a crazy old witch. what next? sweep the beach? empty the ocean by thimblefuls?

much better mindset opening - the Meseta is a powerful expanse... all is laid bare, all is laid bare. all is stretched thin and all man's petty folly and madness is exposed as clear as black rat crap between rice paper sheets. the dark night of the soul before approaching the wondrous fringe of Galicia's mountainous beauty, this fog-soothed peace of the heights. and i'm wondering how far away Casa Anita is? and a shower of gold courtyard bubbling brandywine in a home-made still?

XXXV

   last night's dark rain-front bringing
      morning warm winds,
      walking out under a sliver moon
         that now casts no pilgrim's shadow
            upon the ground ~
yesterday's mind storm,
     a startled crow song silence
              left behind.
         stars haze...
      dawn seeps evenly through
         grey cloud-shaded fields...
and by northern Cantabrian Sea-cast mist, the Meseta plains'
       respiration,
     and some aerially stewed catalyst-mystery
        an atmospherically uncoiled
   barrel-wave crest crashing fogbank Snake emerges
      from los Montes de León,
         the writhing phantom sandworm of Arrakis vanquishes,
in white obliteration, all traces of Astorga behind and
   surges westward the sky long.
      breath suddenly visible,
        where the body broke sweat
           chills,
  much to discover stepping into today's waking fog-churned
        ways

XXXVI

  below towering wisp-headed
      cumulonimbal heights...
         the whale-belly grey
            rain clouded plains ~
groundfog currents shuttle 'n weave
    hillock, vale, mountain fold ~
      burst wing
          wren-flock 'tracers'
            carve
bare jagged winter tree limb
    shapes upon
       a passing white veil breeze

Foncebadón - Ponferrada

hung out with Cincinnati Hospitalero and Mexican Tim and it was late when we left the bar... a few glowing windows waver in the pitch-black and stormy night... yes! a dark and stormy night. wind whipping rain-shrouded phantom fog stallions up the ramshackle village's main drag, and from what i could hear it didn't stop all night.

muggy sleeping in the packed albergue... body heat and hand-wrung laundry steams. Manolo stumbling around sputtering, trying to open windows in the blackness articulately stubs his toes, and it was clear very few in the room were asleep from the soft widespread chuckling

no electricity downstairs in the morning. when it suddenly got jigger-snapped back on a tight-clustered and churning feeding salving plastering frenzy was illuminated. not used to such concentrated human bustle but it was light-heartedly comical like a Marx Brothers farce. opening the front door, light-beams and human sound are sheared away by the tempests without and, to the eyes left in the light, i strode out to disintegrate darkly into wind-lashed rain.

Koala-Susan passed me later writing under the tilted dry arcade of my hat brim. was with José, Alex, Guishermo, Manolo, and Brasileiro Alfonso at the mountaintop towering Iron Cross - thinking of Buckfield and home. from the forests of Buckfield where my Dad has been hunting for over 50 years... where he knows his way around and through, down to stump, sinkhole and boulder... where he steeps himself in Nature's wordless poetry sitting and sunning face beneath aromatic cedars... where the field he learned to drive in is now a tall pine forest... where Wilbur said to Casmire, "If you're so worried about me and the boys, come hunting with us!" and she did... where he lifted a stonewall's granite slab into a throne for his mother to wait upon, upwind of a deer crossing... where as a boy i saw the rusted tea kettle she once hung on a low branch to mark her way around the ridge - then 20 feet up in the air as the tree grew... where November noons, in the abandoned logging cabin we toasted tuna sandwiches on the woodstove's ornate iron griddle and boiled water for blood and soul warming tea... where my Dad, in one of many ways, taught me to walk softly on the Earth... from the forests of Buckfield i've carried a stone, ever since Seville, to cast here as pilgrims have done through the centuries... symbolically leaving burdens and pain behind in the cloud-cleansing mountain heights.

slow descent overlooking mountain-encircled plains below... break in the clouds, solar pulsations, shattered rainbow arc fragments rake mountainsides. blue mountain distance, green mountains near, interlacing valleys fading in white-veiling Autumn rain. descending into El Acebo i remembered a low-ceilinged tienda at the end of town. went there to buy fruit... the old lady shop-keep gifted me a tangerine for coming to see her again. the farm cart with solid wood wheels is still balanced beside the door, and a stump-and-stone bench there for breath and pause.

highlight social time at the Bar! what a kick to run a place like that... a festive refuge in the mountains that marks so many memories. and everybody came on through... Alex / Guishe / José / the ever-smiling Germans from San Martin... the Sherbrooke Québecois sporting his BoSox hat... the streak-haired French woman and her tubby hubby - when they arrived at the Cruz de Hierro this morning someone said, "Mira las Tortugas Ninja Jovenes Mutantes!" 'Teenage Mutant Ninja Turtles!' as that was their look to a 'T' in their dark green poncho-covered backpacks and leggings. the young bartendress kept calling me Caballero. had a coffee and a breakfast anís... and a wine... and setas al ajillo with sausage bits on the bottom of the crock! ...and a bocadillo casero - tuna and tomato on a baguette rolled Monte-Cristo-style in an egg-wash then pan fried... mmmmm. talked mostly with the Nijmegen woman from the León Correos and the crying Cathedral steps - never have got her name... irrelevant to connection. she said she was writing songs to keep the rain away. said i didn't write poems with a purpose. Guishermo said he needs a hooker with spike-heels. one of those 'don't really want to leave' times... had i more time i wouldn't have. i do not regret staying in Foncebadón but El Acebo has a 'timeless haven high in the mountains' feel to it too.

below Riego de Ambrós it was all lush green but for the burnt black tree trunks from a years ago fire. singing 'Ripple,' mind and harp unstrung.

followed the road into Ponferrada under roiling jet-black clouds. thought the albergue was faraway from the center so i checked into a hostal, thinking it would be worth it to be close and visit the Casco Viejo in the light that remains... BUT! after ablutions more torrential rains set in, and for good! not at all amenable to the paseo.

La Galeria Bar - much of the Casco Viejo is getting a facelift and the bar's wall of windows gave views of rainy Templar castle fortifications, rainy scaffolding and rainy yellow back-hoes lustrous against old stone.

bumped into José, Alberto, and Alex and we tried to visit the fortress but they were closing up and José couldn't get his Templario sello... thwarted touristic intentions became a couple rounds of beers.

XXXVII

hill crest sheep bells...
    no two identical baa's bleating out
        nappy woolen throats... shepherd shouts and dog barks
            form a flowing herd,
a living sound-cloud passes
        and sky-clouds mist,
    whitening the valley there into vanish.
footsteps walking on,
    raindrops bead a pissing lingam,
        footsteps walking on,
wind-whipped rain crackles hat-brim ~
        woodsmoke reveals a village down below

XXXVIII

with each mucky mudden trail
    boot step,
        a molecularly gathering rain pearl swells,
swings diadem scintillant on hat brim
        before falling into
           causality ~
in Manjarín, smoldering wet-wood barrel-fire smoke spice
    scents wet whiskers
        and wet clothes ~
rainfall veiled mountain valley, brief cloud breaks...
        rainbow fragmentation embedded
            à l'Excaliber
                in the trees
    for lone wanderers' divine eyes
        to glean

Ponferrada - Villafranca del Bierzo

woke wonderfully naked in clean sheets. left. fairly well knew my way. some changes... major bridge spans being built before that hideously beautiful black ruined factory. (sure the Japanese have a word for hideously beautiful.) then up through the neighborhoods, housing projects, parks... past the white chapel's wall mural of Santa Maria de Compostilla floating over a hill. fat man with two shaggy lap dogs that flutter-footed then stopped warily, flutter-footed then stopped warily at my approach. crossed the roadway into that suddenly familiar suburb - hmm - got a chocolate-full chocolate croissant and YES! there it is! the wildly overgrown yard-side shrub...

    "It's rosemary," she said.
    "That's rosemary?!"
    "Yes."
    "I've never seen it blossoming before."

the shrub by which i met Mirjam for the first time. and the sprig i snipped back then flavored lentils i cooked later in La Faba and shared with German Kristof who exclaimed, "Look! a Monkey!" my eyes searching the trees... "No. Donkey, i mean." a letter away - a continent away. he stayed for free that night, being from the same province as the hospitalero who 'charged' him by having him sing one of their regional songs.

the trail wound out through flat crop plains and flat residential stretches with their kitchen gardens. and suddenly more familiarity - i didn't miss it! Scrooge's "Boy! What day is it?!" despite the phantoms in the sky and mind darkening, i didn't miss it. the mid-street chapel harbinger - that haven has got to be close!

!!!Taberna Mateo!!!

the crimped beer-bottle-cap fly-guard door strings pulled welcomingly aside... had a gentle talk with Encarna, the Boss-Lady. that i stopped here two years ago on a mellow September Sunday afternoon, and had a beer and a tortilla bocadillo outside watching folks cleaning up September-fading kitchen gardens, bundling cornstalks and stoking smouldering brush-pile fires in shrinking rings of grey ash. she's wanting to add a pastelería to the café / bar and get more women working towards their own independence. sends her kids back to her parents in Switzerland, when she can, to expose them to a different life with less engrained machismo. she spoke of the difficulty of getting people to change careless habits - to arrange food on the plates in an appealing way... the cook slopping mess around with an 'O they'll eat it anyway' attitude. a tranquil oasis in Fuente Nuevas.

continued out through the next community - Camponaraya - then out through yellow-and-crimson leaved grapevine plantations where i met the famed Matej Sedmak in 2004... a Peace-Hiker extraordinaire who crossed Pakistani militia-held boarders, befuddling the "Way of the Gun" soldiers by asking simple questions that unbound their conventions. continued on and up, where Matej and i ran into the Aussie women and the Irish girl whose "glad to see the back of you" sarcasm cracked me up. they're the ones who introduced me to Las Crechas years ago - a toast to them! more bright harlequined grapevine hillsides through the hamlet of... Villatuella de Arriba? of which neither i nor the guide have any memory.

strode joyful steps into Villafranca del Bierzo's AVE FÉNIX! the rag-tag albergue burned to the ground once. it has now revived upon its ashes. Jesús de Jato isn't here but his fading-dye-job-brinded wife was receiving and i took her hand saying how happy i was to be here again. the troops arrived - Guishermo / Alex / Manolo - who i'm now calling the Tailless Peacock, he crows and struts so. no idea what he's saying - ever. from the south of Spain where they slur all their words with elision... not even the Spaniards understand him. Alfonso and José were intending to head on to Pereje, but stayed. this is an especial hovelly homey albergue. and Villafranca is a serene refuge masoned against the steep valley-side... mystically Galician in the rain.

only one hospitalera here in the off season - couldn't place the accent. a bit all-knowing and busy-body-ish commanding me to rub on the Arnica - fine. i don't know. i hike 25K and the heel meat bruises. i'm not complaining. and i doubt a salve will take that pain away

saw Koala-Susan and the French Ninja Turtles. they lunched, then did continue on and i accompanied them to the river's edge. rain making the short daylight hours we have even shorter. the Camino contracting around me, the press of birth rippling walls. the man i gave directions to well back in Belorado was shambling down the road. he has an alcoholic's ever-torpored mien.

it would be good to have a meditative albergue in Galicia... a place for one to sit and be still after walking so long on the trail. talking to Encarna earlier, Spain is in an interesting period. not long ago things were difficult here and that depression-era mentality is still alive and well o dammit! i forgot to pay her for my coffee! Encarna! i'll pay the gods!

went in to the Colegiata de Santa Maria de Cluniaco - so differently impressionant than most temples. the canyon-like spacious nave embraced within these enormously pillared walls... above, the interiors of the heavy domes are cobbled and concentrically ringed with small stones. a similar feel to the feel of standing before Saint Pierre's columns in Montpelier arises - a soaring in the belly and lungs elative sensation... a hint of the vertigo stirring. eyes closed, blissful stillness.

Alimentacion - frutas. Farmacia - Vaselina. Albergue - hash-cone passed, soulful whispered conversations, pattering rain.

XXXIX

October cranberry-and-golden grapevine vineyards glow
    from here to Galicia's frontier mountain range
        going pulled-gauze faint with falling rain -
this day of phantom and flesh friends
        stays the mind -
    black crow slices grey sky,
            grey sky reconciles behind...
      cheeks to deep pupils
    burning in kaleidocal leaf-light now,
later to vanish in the cloud-embraced heights

XL

   plucking, plucking... don't have
          a guitar but strums the pen ~
      plucking thick sweet rips from a chocolate-heavy
         chocolate croissant making my
   wine-mossy morning mouth
       smile, plucking rips ~
plucking a 'for to flavor tomorrow's stew'
   rosemary twig from a gangly rosemary
      shrub i once met
         a friend beside,
   now ever to the mind in light lavender bloom ~
plucking one crimson leaf off a
   wall-clung ivy to mark
       the trail guide page ~
   plucking a furry
      seed-headed hay stem
        to rudder tongue and jaw,
          to roll tongue and palate helping
       to remember Here and Now
    when the mind is at maniacal play ~
plucking junk from zipper-tucked folds
     to piss in autumnal rustling
        grey-gold corn rows ~
lapping low-cloud condensation
    from lip whiskers...
       singing a Dylan rambling song

Villafranca del Bierzo - O Cebreiro

remember that stillness in Santa Maria yesterday, and alegría. forgot the tourist-trap aspect of O Cebreiro, the Camino's famed zenith. nowhere to quietly write. will journal tomorrow. i dislike 'catch-up' writing... feels like fan-fingered dog paddling with lead weighted feet.

XLI

    one tire-skidded bare pink flesh
       white twig-bone snapt
          organ sac elsewhere
            mouse,
splayed upon the tar freshly steams,
   untouched by boot or crow.
Nature's fine manicured nails
  on deathcurl paws
     peel the four wayward
        winds from Galician cloudy skies

XLII

dead and loving it!
   blow my pound of ashes off the cliffs
      of Finistera
         wrapt in
potassium, sodium, and clove spice
   to explode flare-firework cascades…
      another flash wings across the long galaxial night

XLIII

in her perfection,
    the season's softest rain...
        spiny chestnut burr seams dilate, prime...
            for sun, time, rain, chill night's quiver and rift,
mother-of-pearl lined setaceous petals slowly open talonly
    to reveal one more burnished mahogany hull.
        another
        nut
        falls
upon another ending Autumn's trunk-ring respired ground,
    five hundred years
        of serrate shade
    and 'all in all's due time' fruit thumping
        upon earthen mould and earthen mind,
            all in all's due time

XLIV

the cold crashing-wave-edged universe expands ~
    against this brief
        sun-warmed earth face i feel the flesh fringe
            fray and retain
    with cosmos' osmosis.
breathing from the belly's coal-ember core
        to Ave Fénix'
            crumble brick walls and away...
the only one awake
    peeking beneath
        god's sheets.

        *

cloud-wrapt green Galician mountains surround,
    rain patters these
        Villafranca del Bierzo
            steep stone streets

Villafranca del Bierzo - O Cebreiro - Sarria

left Ave Fénix and Villafranca in the darkness and the rain - rain rivulet stone streets flashing precipitant in the ochre lantern light... thinking how! how i could live here... hearthside warm stone, mist and green. another chaplet of rustic slate villages tucked against interlacing mountainsides, rushing river serpentines below, sound of the rain pattered stones. Pereje, Trabadelo... wooly mammoth chestnut trunk-lined trail.

stopped at the hippy albergue in La Faba for fire, bench, and warming wine. gay Argentinean and German hospitaleros... high-pitched and congenial. it was rather too rustic an abode for the Argentinean. i didn't understand much of what he said but he described an ocean goddess / Maria ritual in the north of South America where bygone gods blend with new... on the beach all day in silence, dressed in white, holding flowers... at sunset - flowers cast to the tide and candles set afloat. then begins the all-night Babylonian baccanale, which at sunrise ceases.

climbing out of la Faba through layers of color / light / shade / shadow / cloud / mountain / green pasture / yellow poplars in mountain valley folds / pied fern-death hillsides -- the coppery maroons and yellows against grey-green undergrowth banding dramatically when sunlight slips through the clouds.

stepped into the O Cebreiro albergue to the ear-splitting cacophonics of Jackhammers, Generators and those Bowel Rolling Cement Mixing Machines... renovations underway... and walked out. no way. spent too much for a tiny room but i couldn't handle Jackhammers.

inside the church - cold. pebble embedded flip-flop soles make unsettling clack-'n-grind noises on the stone floor. outside - vistas of low cloud-bellies scraping the near mountaintops, darkening here while sight's distance is bright.

that was yesterday... oi. today - out by 7:15H and i was terrified!

STYGIAN BLACK MOUNTAINS... mist veils falling from an inky sky... that posted article i didn't read back at the Ave Fénix:

Lobos: No Madrugas!

(Wolves: do not set forth in the early morn!)

it freaked me out even though i was on the Liñares road and not a shadowy sylvan path. coal-bright wolf eyes pierce imagination... i turned and went back inside until 8H.

stopped for a coffee in Liñares. a chestnut and snail gathering old codger slogged wetly in for a fortifying tumbler of red wine and fried pork rinds... his streaming oilcoat steams with the rank of goat... caracoles escaping his satchel. a Spanish couple, too quickly defrocking at the bar, break the snaps off their cheap impermeables. curses and laughter. then bleary-eyed Rambling-Alex who slept in the French Turtles' room and rose so early... sooo not like the Spaniard room, he grumbled, who sleep in.

as i left, the rain kicked in in earnest - a patter-trancing rainfall massaging mind. all but for the torso wet, smiling, and would have rather been nowhere else.

up the steeply pitched climb to Col San Roque - grand statue of a traditionally cloaked peregrino bending shoulders to and clasping hat against the constant wind that historically blows here... and presently i mime him against today's whipping rain. a café is there at the high-point belvedere and in the parking lot, the French relay bus the telegrinos are using was idling warmly and full, few storm trekkers... the Gauloise-smoking chauffeur smiles and waves.

along the trail i couldn't help stopping to break up the twig-and-leaf snaggles the rain water pushes into dams. the will of the theoi nomioi within. heavy rain falling from the trees when the wind gusted, and gust it did. these mighty-trunked chestnuts, which i stood once before in holy palms open to holy sky awe, i stand before now once again... honored old beasts in time.

met a cow herd changing pastures coming down the trail... curious cows stepping close to sniff cavernous-sinus whooshing sounds at me and stare. effulgent emerald green pastures... mid-hill hugging trail... surrounding mountains pulsing white, fade, and vanish with passing fogs.

the string of hewn earth-bone Galegan hamlets... Montán, Furela, Pintín, Calvor, Camiño. on her grey porch a thick peasant woman wearing a flour-powdered cindery apron hacks kindling wood with an axe... the sodden-vegetation muffled sound. before one stone and wood-beam staggered veranda, flush with all the colors geraniums could ever long to be, i was florally mesmerized under drenching unfelt rain.

the steep main road up through Sarria's Casco Viejo is alive with private albergues and pilgrim info shops. this is the closest to Santiago where one can begin walking the Pilgrimage and still receive the blessèd Compostela, still be spiritually reprieved from purgation's hot chains. over a corner bar at the top of high cement-slab stairs i got an 8E room. when i entered, the dueña was cleaning behind an either scrubbed clean or brand new plancha. a bevy of abuelitas seated, watching, supervising... telling her to attend to me. "Momento!" she snaps. hey. it ain't me, babe, who's telling you to rush. no no no... it ain't me. while waiting i checked the time for the first time since Triacastela - 17:30! had no idea it was so late... the timelessness beneath grey skies.

while searching for the alimentacion i bumped into the Frenchman from Lyon i'd walked with earlier in the day... coldly impersonal at first, then back-slap laughing. he didn't recognize me bathed, hatless and uncloaked... the morphology of Man. friendly woman in the grocery store helped me root out where Spain's version of 'Savon de Marseilles' was hidden. deep in Galicia now and all a more difficult to understand Galego patois.

20:30H - and i'm heading up to my room whose window opens to the high cement-slab staircase reverberating earlier with the sounds of heavy pilgrim's boots and walking sticks clacking in the drum brush whisperin' rain.

made a well-stacked sub. drank some wine. wondering frankly, finishing this poem, what could be better? what could be better than now? washed clothes and the sweat-soured windbreaker... all now a-drape on the furniture to perhaps dry. billion-fingered rain thrums the sky-light.

XLV

the universe is sight-white around
        save whispering fog misted
    black pines' emergence and fade ~
        shudder wolven fear felt in the bone marrow
          setting out into night-veiled dawn,
            now gone ~

      *

a wind-surged phantom stallion herd
    courses   gallops   rages
        crushes skull to smear me
sweetly trodden brow and mind
    against this Galician mountainside home,
      home,   the soul's cradle comfort home.
    one golden window in stacked schist and stone.
walking wrapt in pied fall
    through maroon and amber fern-death hillside fields
    and growths of silver-grey broom
        which in summertime sings with
      yellow-nectared blooms...
    rich yellow nectared blooms
the setting moon oft mines,
    alembics,
        and Li Po-ly sips to shine

XLVI

and then quite frankly sick of me,
    i piss divinely wine back into water into
    the eternal ceramic bowled sea...
        a silly little drunken joke
            th' evangelist let slip from history...
  that thine and thee is the miracle,
    that sunrise is the pea,
        that he who called the Almighty papa
            shits and stinks and snores and soars
        Pavarottial as me.
    that all   All   ALL is deific!
        from Einsteinian, Euclidian, Augustinian mind,
to the liver-slab-flapping cow-cunt queefage of an Argentinian
                bovine...
        all is deific and all is deific and
        does not we un-divine.

        *

a rented stone-room slumber
    above this shoddy bar
    in checkered sheets,
        handsink washed clothes
            dry in night window wind
  to dress me simply walking westward
    clothes, skin, flesh, bone, marrow,
        th' universe-wide whispering
            alegría heart's glee

Sarria - Portomarín

standing at the bar this morning having a coffee and watching thick pear-shaped raindrops spark the street-channeling cascades... unabating and amazing. shin deep run-off torrents! how does this hillside town not wash away?! stepped out the front door and was immediately soaked. down the back of the hill... peregrinos coming around the other side... suspected taxi-grinos from the train station carefully tip-toeing on hummock and rock. i sloshed quickly by. come on people! with 25K ahead of you in this rain, now is no time to prance dryly on stones.

a lot of head down and straight onward, but in such an elative mood... powerfully, hot muscularly moving through landscape and storm. these days of long rains make Galicia, make the dense green and mist-rolled mornings in the heights... this is part of the Galician embrace.

trail steepened sharply. i took time to now and again lay my brow against rough wet oak and chestnut trunks shadowing the path... oak and chestnut trees swollen massy with earth, air, storm, season, and bright time... another concentric ring respires with me in cellulosic mind.

for much of today's etapa the trail ribboned along at mid-hill height, tunneled in viridescent pattering. and it was a river! socked feet squashing in the boots, with each step aware of squishy toes... the systole / diastole of warm boot water seething round the ankles. slow realization that these are path-rivers of excrement gathering pasture run-off, washing all the cow, chicken and goat feculence from hamlet lanes and hillsides, all the hay-refuse shoveled and squeegeed out of first floor stables, all shit-water squashing through toes and socks. probably no problem but i'm glad i don't have any open sores.

Vilei, Barbadelo, Mercado de Serra, Peruscallo... small agro / husbandry chestnut and oak huddled villages... unchanged but for collapses' occasional repair. Morgade, Ferreiros, Moimentos, Parrocha... crumbling cement-and-cobbled embossments upon a hillside, black slate roofs spattering wet sparks, a young dog bounding full-on at me - of him unafraid. i know Galicia is in his blood. he needed some love, i needed some love, or Love needed us both... pet him for a while, then he followed me jumping at the flapping rain cape. warm cave-lair cafés thick with shadows, backpacks, and disembodied foreign voices appear. the one where Mirjam asked me, in precise German syllables, "How was your rosemary and potatoes?" was particularly Middle Earthen.

to circumvent a raging whitewater-washout impasse i meandered directionless through sloppy mud and slippery vegetation to a commune with a hound of Hell, viciously unthrilled to see me... asked an age-bent peasant couple in matching green plastic boots the way... "Arriba! Arriba!" semi-toothless and smilingly pointing "Arriba! Arriba!"

didn't get vertigo this time crossing that crazy Portomarín bridge but should have zigzagging to it. this way and that again, this way and that. joined a cow herd down the stonewall edged road... advancing oddly, small-ly, among the great clopping hoofed beasts.

went directly to the first hostal and, despite the 'no clothes washing in the sink' sign, i washed my clothes post-haste in the sink - and with walking stick, desk and chair i rigged up a drying rack. guide is soaked and i left it on the heater to proof. thankful i had no poetry notes in my hip pack as it was drenched through.

through the window i saw Mexican Daphne and her 'rice rain' sister, but after yesterday's double etapa most faces are new. lot of peregrinos arriving late-day and haunting the dry arcades surrounding the plaza. they must have waited for the rain to never stop.

stamped my Credenciale in the empty echoey church. nearly 18H. looking forward to being in my room listening to roof rain.

XLVII

  crumbled stonewall arms
      embrace a green
          weed raptured
              October garden...
from black frost-rot ragged vegetation
        one blood-red tomato hangs tantaline
            over tangerine calendula eyes.
     wind whipped rain crackles hat brim,
        walking smiles by

Portomarín - Palas de Rei

nervous this morning. dried my boots over the electric heater all night. probably not a wise thing to do to leather. amazed at how Hermes-heels light they were! amazed at how tight they were! thought i screwed up fearing too-tight foot abrasions, but they quickly stretched.

the rain is conscious. it stopped overnight, then as it heard me rousing it commenced pounding on the sky-light again.

a day full of memories. passed through Gonzar, a scrap of a hamlet where i stayed two years ago and met simpatico people. German Hippy with his friendly dog who slept under the stairway, the French Girl i honed peace with unraveling the differences between discernment and judgement, Mirjam was there, and the non-stop talking Aussie who was getting sour on the Camino. trail mainly followed along the carretera until the bridge where the two guys behind me began whistling 'Darth Vader's Theme,' and then...

HORRIBLE! The Aviporto!! never have i smelled such stench fetor in my entire life! NEVER! and i hope never to again... some guano fertilizer processing factory's green storage silos olfactorily overflowing. don't know if it's new or if the wind blew the other way last time by here but it was wretched. backpack laden, i lumberingly ran past to make my escape.

more copse and hillside growths of Enormous Platonic Chestnut Ideals... no shades on cave walls here. grey stone enclaves, gentle trail, occasional showers, a constant hat brim flipping wind. beneath the first sight of the Galician eucalyptus trees, an Irish Red Setter sitting in the middle of a rippling road, twitch-ears listening to the lyrics the leaves make with rain. interesting cruceiro with Madonna and Child on one side, skull and crossbones on the other, and carved into the base were the tools of the local trades... advertising in the old-time way.

went into Palas de Rei's ironically drab municipal albergue. two Americans came in during ablutions. couldn't place a regional accent. Alberto's here and weary after taking the road to San Xil but ending up instead in much-further Samos... and Lukas the tent-Pole, uncharacteristically cluttered with a feisty dog and two Brasileiras! thought he'd be well ahead by now.

few familiar faces passing outside the café window... saw a man with the blackest beard i briefly glimpsed days before by the windrainfog whipped peregrino statue at Col San Roque.

at least the morning rain was warm. this afternoon front that has moved the rain away is cold-winded.

Palas de Rei - Arzúa

it was 7H before i finally checked time and got out of bed. rolled up my kit and went downstairs to where the American couple was breakfasting in the austerity cold neon light reflected off bare cement walls makes... and Lukas the tent-Pole was rustling on a bench. i'm copping the sense one Brazilian gave warmth and succor the ground did not provide. he said some crackpot got into the albergue in Portomarín, started lighting matches and tossing them on peoples' sleeping bags. Lukas slowly woke first to the smell of smoke, then to the sight and feel of way too close flames!

walked darkly out through more of the tree shaded stone-home clustered villages of Galicia... Carballal, San Xulian, Coto, Leboreiro's plastic bloom blooming tombwalls leveed concentrically around the church, Furelos... gaping black stable doors billowing white bovine exhalations and steam from the backs of the great damp beasts. no rain yet, but i took out my poncho in preparation. the tell-tale omen is that last night's cold is gone. the warmer air boding rain.

much familiarity... the bridge where the wheelchair fakirs were begging that they made their way from Jerusalem and needed just a little more money to get to Santiago. the 'All' that has not changed throughout time... storytelling beggars, meretricious trinkets disintegrating in the fist, Christians seeking sancta sanctorum crannies shrining splinters of the Rood... and these pilgrim feet on the wrong road entering Melide, getting directions from a man with a plow.

through blinding and deafening rain i searched the center looking for grub. found a bar. a few tumblers of wine, pulpo - the octopus arms boiled until tender then sautéed with oil and paprika and topped with crunchy salt... a chorizo bocadillo... then back out through aria-ly emerald landscapes.

stopped. the flashback hand-painted sign... 'BAR 30M - Acceso al Camino,' as it was off-piste. chubby dueña with an 18-month-old boy and bar / grocery in her front livingroom. gentle relaxation. she started directing me to the shortcut back as i was leaving and i told her that not only did i remember the way, i remembered she had a toddling little girl and was pregnant with the cherub hollering now. asked if when i returned she'd have another and she cradled her head laughing and pushed me out the door.

one farmer calling out to his cows... they recognized him and came running. running! a running cow is a poor picture of grace. we talked a bit surrounded by washed out upper-field mud, ankle deep in the road. 'This isn't normal.' not Summer's heat, nor Autumn's torrential rains... not normal.

A Peroxa, Boente... grapes on leafless vines hang arbor-wired over a faded green door. Castañeda's kiwi vines pend white petaled blooms and testicular fruit. tunnel under the highway was totally flooded but i found my circumvential way easily around flood and town. traipsed into Arzúa and - to a pension with me... a pension with no heat, a grey-windowed balcony and high 'cockle closing pearl comfort round me' walls. chatty receptionist. she loves Springsteen, el Boss. "Me encanta, el Boss!"

the best pizzeria on the Camino is opening at 20:30H!

for sudden downpour driving rain i ducked into Bar El Teatro Mágico for a coffee and a dram (que j'en boirai, oui, oui, oui, jusqu' à mon plaisir) ...and found myself in mutual déjà-vu before the silver-line lion painted upon a mirrored wall... 'Cabrón, Cabrón, Cabrón, Cabrón' song sounding like the Chili Peppers. by the window walks the Austrian who slept in the bunk above me last night and fabricated a crazy-intricate clothesline i half expected would floss his teeth while he slept, so Rube Goldbergly pullied and counter-weighted it was... must be an engineering student.

compaction, compression, the weight of these days ending... and the sky is blue. that's actually up for debate as i haven't seen it since ...?... 'and the grass is an un-sun-bleached emerald green' is more accurately the balm of equanimity... and the grass is an un-sun-bleached emerald green.

XLVIII

walked out into dawn-yet-untinctured night
    using all senses save sight to make my way ~
        the soul tendrils outwardly touching...
            echo-locate foot falls sounding close
                chestnut and oak friends,
        malty hay fermentation,
           fresh morning cabbage scent,
           and the sound of water rushing stone
all shawl me in Galician mind ~
    watching mice silhouettes
        drip beads down slate-roofed horreo corner seams...
classic cartoon sun smilingly leaps to bright day
        and from stonewall, refuse pile and wire cage
           a rooster chorus responds moments before
                returns the gentle rain ~
anima mundi innerly-lit green pastures surround
one fey late-October raspberry bramble bloom,
        which sometimes blooms like a poem...
            for the sake of stopping and steeping in beauty,
                and not of fruit

XLIX

storm-snapped
    slender-finger-leafed eucalyptus branch tip
        disembodiedly
           paws at the trail with the breeze,
tangles of eucalyptus bark peel roll by,
    boot-heel-crunched eucalyptus nuts,
        eucalyptus menthol musk brightens sinuses...
we are deep in Galicia now, you and i ~
        warily balancing on tortoise-back boulders to ford a
            raging stream...
        heavenly! heavenly!

                    to inhale this un-sun-bleached
                         meadow green...
        let it rain and drench me crack 'n loin,
            let silver drop sparks flash trail-running streams,
                let its mythic fogs roll,
                    mossed-stone chapel bell-towers toll,
            let cemeteries' death-muck seep and feed nearby kitchen
                            garden
                peasants' hunger needs, let it rain
                    and wash all Now's pink to hoary child-kind's
fingers, ears, toes, nose, and precious brow clean,
        let it rain,   let it heal,
              let it rain   let it rain   let it heal   let it rain

L

left the long-unused blue sunscreen tube
   on a leaky hostal windowsill, pooling rain.
now, pissing in wet moss,
     lightening the bladder sac
         to birdsong arias
             and undertones,
     10,000 hedgehogs' horror
         balled up beneath a sigh-limbed
             chestnut tree.
"N'ayez pas peur. C'est moi." makes me smile.
      but if they unfold
         i'll frikin' flee

Arzúa - Santiago de Compostela

woke. dressed in clothes barely dry for the heatless room and damp skies. had a smilingly served coffee in a neon-lit bar while the storm tossed tree-tops around the plaza. wound down into pitch dark and mist, following the will of a stonewall-lined lane through the silent village and out into rain pattered fields. an invisibly hooded peregrino with a flashlight ahead of me, like a phosphorescently tendriled creature of the deep... we exchanged polite Spanish syllables. ten minutes later, she... "Do you speak English?" it was Koala-Susan! stumbled along a long time in the fog-ghosting flashlight beams, but ah! to speak English smoothly. talked of our trails, sights, scents, mind. her shoes are Keens which use that Massai technology. they don't seem to have much ankle support but she's never had a blister and bought them new. will look into those surely, thinking back on the months of gauzes and tapes.

she stopped. i continued the winding forest trail on to Santa Irene, where i did... yes... spend the night in a Casa Rural 'two years ago.' in a roadside bar with a clapboard cabin feel i fortified with several jam-jar wines and a crock of lentils. deliveries coming hand-trucked in - beers, breads, hams, cans.

left feeling good. a horse cantered up to me from the other side of the fence in apple tree shade. she had picked her pasture-side clean of fruit and spoke to me in silent eye. i tossed over an apple which she bit and chewed, turned, bit and chewed. listening to chomping's satisfaction i tossed over a few more windfall apples before proceeding on.

trail serpentined through oak and pine... then through mainly eucalyptus woods and fern growth groundcover. intense cloying-to-sinus scent of forest-fired eucalyptus trunks i imagine must torch long into the night, so flush with the flammable oil are bole and leaf.

stopped for a 'blood of the peregrino' tipple in Lavacola... yes, Lavacola. the etymological roots are the same in many languages, lenguas, linguas, langues... the streams running through Lavacola are where medieval pilgrims would traditionally stop to wash their reeking medieval asses before presenting themselves before the tomb-shrine of St. James. this fact of gamy human flesh is what actually led to the botafumeiro ceremony at the end of the High

Mass... pounds of incense had to be burned post-eucharist or the Holy Spirit his dovely self would have dropped out dead from the Godhead!

a long day. strode physically strong through all the up and downing, but innerly exhausted. scattered mind and focussed. cold molasses fatigue heavy in the eyes. blackhole gravitationals contracting far-shot starlight into mustard seed DNA helices once again... Lord Shiva dancing the Tandava.

AND I MADE IT! i made it. complete with mood swings and mind-trash to celebrate my birthday tomorrow! back at Monte de Gozo the black clouds were no longer distant and, under pounding rain, i crossed a rusted steel bridge into residential Santiago... into the long uninteresting schlep to the Casco Viejo... the old city presenting itself with cinereous granite fronts and shadow-sheltering stone arcades. slowly i circled the Cathedral and with that emotional Roy bloodline... teared up with magnified memory before each facade, dwelling on the past five calendar months and the timelessness of mind.

went to the Pilgrim's Office to register... bitchy pilgrim chic giving the secretary a hard time because she couldn't provide train information. honey, the tourist office is down the street... yelling here won't change that. i received a flimsy second-rate certificate of showing up and breathing instead of the Latin Compostela because i said my goal wasn't 'religious' ...which soured my mind for thirteen seconds and which now makes me smile. that that makes any moment, any of the eternal footsteps from Arles less valid... if showing up and breathing is suitable for Gautama, Jimmy's in good company.

went up to the Girasol... Boss Lady wasn't there but the Rear Guard Daughters took care of me. went to my Barakal Café for a wine and pimientos de Padrón - and more than half of them were powerfully picante. owner said, ' "They say" when it rains there are more spicy ones.' 'they' are right today.

found my barbers 'from two years ago' and got the best coif! no way with my limited vocabulario can i describe how i want my hair cut... and those warming waiting room chairs chuckle when i shrug and say in Spanish, 'more short than now.' looked around for a shirt but shops are closing up. and my counter-acquaintance at the Dolmen wasn't working. tomorrow after the Mass i'll stop by again to buy a few azabache trinkets. the single-decade silver scallop-shell-beaded chaplet i bought there two years ago, Mémère looped around her wedding ring for safety so it wouldn't get lost among her deathbed's sheets...

Santiago under rain... few people in the streets. somber.

went to the marisco strip of restaurants on the pedestrian street in the shadow of the spires - reading window menus under pounding rain, trying to decide... rolled pants to the knees but the deluge didn't rush me. stone-street streams coursing soothe my bruised sandaled feet.

LI
muck-rot maroon
    eucalyptus leaf-fall forest floor,
        dying-down bronze fern fronds
            tack with whispering wind shreds...
    tendriled currents tumbled low from the green canopy above
        cool today's humid brow,
            a rain pool ripples.
this last day on the trail...
    Santiago Cathedral Spires
        will brighten my eyes tonight,
thighs and feet will know such ease
    tomorrow morning,
        maroon and bronze and transmutatively shimmering
            green eucalyptus ease

Catedral de Santiago de Compostela

yes, foggy from a late Las Crechas night... got drinks at the downstairs bar and squeezingly sidled my way through the crowd to sit closer to the sesshun. English peregrino said, "Careful, wall's wet. Rain seepage." i replied, "Brother, I've been wet for weeks." plus it was refreshing in that smoke bath. jamming music. didn't check the time rolling home...

foggy from a late Las Crechas night, but Buddha-Alegra Hound watching me through the bushes with a crooked smile.

got to the Cathedral early but there was no need. a few English, Spanish, and French tour groups passed by, but by late October there aren't the estival vacationing crowds. a different energy altogether - mellow, solemn. the nun who led the pre-mass responsorial practice runs tried to get people to sing loud, but who can remember Latin responses? and it felt like the officiating priest was trying to be rejoiceful. those moments with the Botafumeiro, however, were emotive. flickering flames glint behind silver grates swinging high... sweet smoke, organ, song, and long reflections.

went back to my Barakal Café for short crocks of chorizo al vino and gambas al ajillo and wine... tired from a not that restful sleep... looking forward to siesta.

a phase ending...

went shopping and got a Navarra blue buttondown, socks, and stylin' 'Café Noir' sneakers. so funny! so happy pacing around the store with sneakers, not flip-flops or boots on. what a backflipping feel to wear sneakers! went to see my friend at the Dolmen... bought a smooth modern silver and azabache ring and that's that.

haven't seen the troops.

those tenderest chipirones last night... flash fried on the plancha in garlic oil with a few boiled potatoes... mmmmmm... and the

Azpilicueta - 2003 Crianza blending Tempranillo and Graciano Mazuelo varietals... ahhh.

LII

left a roadside bar well-lubed with light red wine glasses drained,
    tortilla francesa con queso
        on plancha-toasted split bread
        and sausage-y lentil soup...
a simple feast after 15 of a 40K last
    day's march to Compostela. trail banged
        a right away into a 500 years
        ago stone village, mossily grown,
rushing mountain-water streams
    singing to all ages' ears who walk here...
        unbleached by sun for the long weeks of
        rain, a sweetgrass green pasture's
fence wraps an apple tree, palings rotten at the damp-loam base,
    and she saunters towards me in stranger-angel unawares...
        one flickering cable-cord muscled
        chestnut mare making her solid hoof
on wet ground way... and in the manner
    of pre-speech beasts, suddenly my
        mind awakens
        to her fenced pasture-side picked clean...
picked clean. and with love in bending backpack weighted
    back, with love in reaching ground-ward,
        with love in touching the rain-cool windfall fruit
        i toss an apple over the barbed wire
which with large lips and large teeth and
    opposable-thumb-talented tongue the handless have
        developed, she bit and chewed
        and raised her chestnut maned

ebon-eyed head nodding
    thankfulness, one hoof scraping thankful runes
        upon wet earth three times.
        three apples
and a few moments of eternal time.
    Now, Santiago Cathedral spires are night-bright behind me,
        the dark Hostal de los Reyes Catholicos
        hotel terrace corner finds me looking
sunset westward at pale peach clouds whose
    direction is no longer destination-bound!
        the heart-mind wings,
        birthday meal of the best garlic-oil-crisped
chipirones settles into bowels...
    new shirt, new socks, new sneaks, new ring...
        bagpipes echo out
        a stone archway,
a few coins in the black leather change pouch
    clink out busker's tips
        strolling to Las Crechas'
        tobacco-cloud-cured wood beam and
stone walled cave for Guinness pints and whiskies,
    and opiate smoke rings...
        not bandaging feet in the morning.
        not Vaseline-ing the rash-inclined crotch.
not cross-lacing boots. not breakfasting
    on fruit to fire the body's furnace for another
        30K of re-learning that each
        duality-heresy, each bitter-sweet twinge unbinds in
awareness's open hands...
    and between pocket watch and Cathedral Spire time
        it's midnight now, now where
        the hell's that tambourine man

LIII

tracing eyes over ornate illumined
    Baroque Cathedral Spires
        crinkle-blinks the late-night mind.
            when light-waves suddenly ebb into
                vanish,
pupils pool...
    dark shadow towers against a darker sky
        untouched by low streetlights'
            amber glow ~
                tone sharp 1/2 ton bell tolls
four quarters for the coming hour's call,
    and one baritone bell bangs 1a.m...
        cigaret lighter flames flicker
            coven-huddled faces
                hunkered on Praterías Square's
shout-wide staircase... drunk or stoned
    or just young loud voices talk, sing, and throng,
        'nothing new under the sun or moon' conversations echo
            against the ancient carved and foot-worn
                plaza stone...
all whisper to song
    watery human sound rippling
        in this stone plaza bowl,
            whirlpool eddies turning,
                churning billion year old starlight's last scintillant
                breath...
song talk whisper
    guitar footsteps shout and laughter
        swirling whirl 'n mael storm's eye
            reminding mind the inevitable inevitability of smooth
            quiet seas...
                the halcyon-hearted tempest teachings of the Shiva-
                seas

Finistera

not enough days remain for me to walk to Finistera this second time. and there's no 10H bus on Saturdays... 14-14:30H is departure time.

uneventful ride - grouchy alkie-face from Belorado on the bus. went to the hostal i stayed at in July. warm and hazy by the sea. ablutions - sort of. just washed my socks and bagged the rest to ¡burn baby burn! bought newspaper tinder and bocadillo fixin's for tomorrow on the cliffs. O Fragón of the forgotten credit card was closed... and La Galeria looks closed too. Bar A Galeria / Rúa Real 25 / Finistera. must write my thanks.

stopped in a shady port-side bar for a drink... elaborate espresso machine. '30-40 years old,' he says. the hand-pump lever i've see before, but through the grate below... rippling blue gas flames heat the reservoir!

on the rocks by the boat-slip listening to sloshing and seagulls... the inner-harbor looks dirty from the rain. Cee flooded four times in less than a month. shellfisherman / harvesters are screwed - with all the refuse washed out to the shores, mariscos have suffocated and much of the shoreline is dead. saw many burnt-out regions along the bus route. forest fires and flooding undo a land.

O Fragón opened at 20H! and i'm here with a Pagos de Quintana - Ribera del Duero... a nose like sawing cherry wood in barnyard sunlight. probably my last meal in Spain. shouldn't bother being frugal now... had this appetizer here in July. menu says 'fried cheese' - a slab of plancha-grilled smoked provolone drizzled with caramel sauce. the pulpo, still paprika-ed and coarse salted, but hit with olive oil to make it shine. garlic roasted besugo. and whatever mystery word i thought was some exotic shellfish... is a baked potato.

LIV

three ice-cubes
   in the last whiskey glass sip
      gleam the same molten
         gold as ensconced mesh-mantle gas
      barroom chimney globes.
Costa da Morte sea surrounds...
   Fistera peninsula, sea-bound...
      not a July seagull chortles,
      a dog bays,
   Saturday drunks bray,
      the hundred and fifty nights i've been away
         blur,
      blackhole, germinate,
and bloom in the tingling earth-flesh
      of my sauntering soles.
      the meditative 'bring me here or bust'
         Montaignes Noires stone,
            having worn the pants' pocket-fabric threadbare,
will be fist-cast to the sea tomorrow from jagged Fistera cliffs...
   a runic action feasted with a final chorizo tomato onion cheese
   bocadillo,
      watching fire smoke
         rise beside the rippling blue sea

Cabo Finisterra, Costa da Morte

woke at what i thought was late. went to the German-Bartended café by the water. one Aussie couple from back in Puente la Reina was there! they told me of the 'Fall behind' time change that made it a bit earlier. walked out, hot, dripping sweat, collecting dry broom-twigs along the 3K trail to the cliffs. climbed down through steep gorse and sharp stones to a flattish boulder and slowly assembled my tinder, newspaper and stick pyre. before a plane of sea and a plane of sky i burned t-shirt, underwear, pants, and the SPF magic-fabric button-down that's been with me for three Caminos. built my fire, burned my clothes, built my bocadillo and ate.

this afternoon one boot drying on the windowsill leapt down into an unassailable alley low below. will knock the other off the sill to join them later tonight.

wandered the port a while and went down to see if the Galeria had opened... nope. done for the season. a memory closed. came up to the Celtic Cerveceria near my hostal. mismatched Celtic strings and gazelle horns and tribal African masks on the walls. there was a raging fiesta last night in my hostal bar that did not stop! and i'm sure not to sleep tonight too, knowing i want to wake up early. thus begins my initial conveyance back home... Finistera - Santiago - Santiago - Madrid by about 22:30H. i have become freight.

the three Czechs i met back in Pirineos' shade just came into the bar for rounds of congratulations and well wishes. they said i was the first pilgrim they met on their journey, and here we are at the end of things.

LV

against stained-glass radiant blue sky planes...
    the cat-fur-satin sheen
        pine needles share with beasts,
    purple heather swarmed in gold gorse blooms
      and tangerine lichened stone
        form the frame for it all...

    *

i found my Fistera steep ocean-cliff
   boulder niche
      to sit slanted upon and watch the blue sea churn
         cream spume, to build my
   twinkle little star fire upon, and
   the clothes that clothed me for
so many miles and minds to here burn
   white smoke smiles into the cloudless...
      chorizo cheese onion red tomato tucked into a
         white baguette fold...
      licking fingers, face colors in the sun,
stirring sticky polypropylene residue
white broomwood ashes cool. strange sounds...
   a flipper-powered seal pack
      bellyflops solid-hollow whacking glee
         splashes against the surface
      o' the far-reaching sea...
   currents more real than compass rose arrows
weave life's bind
   in unbinding the elegant weave...
      the holy helix moot as mud if not unlaced
         and let to vagabond the rails

Fistera - my bed in Cambridge, Massachusetts...

an early morning bus to Santiago... a morning bus full of loud schoolkids who got louder as the bus got stuck in traffic within sight of the school and the driver wouldn't open the doors - "Abre! ABre! ABRe! ABRE!"

a last lunch on Praza Obradoiro... bought the International Herald Tribune and headed to the bus station. mellow bus mindstate. working with the acceptance of continually working within... the halcyon-hearted storm.

through a prophylactic bus window - half-moon hanging over

golden poplar valley plains... garden refuse brush-smoke corkscrews the sky... mountains fading hazy blue.

glad to see Black Beard this morning at the Spreken-zie-Deutsch Spaniard Sailor's bar. he gave me the tip for Hotel Conchita at the Legazpi subway terminal, here in Madrid. directions were precise, thankfully! as there were nothing but apartments and condos by the bus station. 43E is more than BB said 'Conchita' cost but less than i was willing pay for convenient ease.

Legazpi is seedy. nothing open but this bar. a dusty humid night... soot in the air tangible in the hand when i rub cheek and brow.

tomorrow i'll be home... should be in Cambridge by 19:30H - 7:30 p.m., that's 1:30 in the morning to my flesh and mind. crossing my fingers there's a peach lambic in the fridge.

i should sleep like a lamb in a wolf-less land.

LVI

below Plaza Obradoiro's ten stone steps,
   ten stone steps down to an angle
      owning so many baroque Cathedral facade backdrops of
      hands-to-hips Here I conquer!
         Here I have arrived!
            photos poised.
down these ten stone steps I find my final meal ~ my final cold
   Ribeiro tinto washing raciones through
      flesh and mind sustaining me the long bus ride
      to late-night Madrid ~
tortilla de patatas
   tooth-picked cubes, marbled
      chorizo caseiro sliced
      and slipped onto a
         paprika-stained white ceramic plate clacks against
         a burnished platter piled with
pimientos de Padrón, fried to wilt and sea-salt-crunch
   perfection,
      clacking against another burnished platter of
      plancha-crisped chipirones
seared to the miraculous switch
   between crust and tender, and hearty bread
      to mop thy ambrosic residues...
   caramel caramelo frosted
      café solo,
         too short to dissolve the sugar-packet dose.
the thick liqueur lacily graces
   a dipped silver demitasse spoon and
      sated tongue
      gratefully, gratefully, the long one
         more bus, metro, hotel, taxi,
            plane, taxi way home,
               to sleep like a lamb in a wolf-less land.

Afterward

Holding those "ages of littoral-haunting barefoot blistered souls" in hallowed mind now, not only is it my aim that <u>Sons of Thunder</u> and <u>Autumn on the Trail to Santiago</u> express one great and seasons-wide breath of the Camino de Santiago experience, but it is this pilgrim's wish that these two works, side by side, be a Memory Palace... be a liquid-lensed looking glass to step through for I am intent upon haunting these paths long after my flesh is elementally returned to earth, water, wind, and late-night campfire flames.

Jim

Cambridge, Massachusetts

February, Anno Santo 2011